METAPHOR

NEW PROJECTS BY

SMITHSONIAN INSTITUTION PRESS, WASHINGTON, D.C., 1982

METAPHOR

CONTEMPORARY SCULPTORS

VITO ACCONCI, SIAH ARMAJANI, ALICE AYCOCK,
LAUREN EWING, ROBERT MORRIS, DENNIS OPPENHEIM

HOWARD N. FOX

HIRSHHORN MUSEUM AND SCULPTURE GARDEN
SMITHSONIAN INSTITUTION

Hirshhorn Museum and Sculpture Garden
Smithsonian Institution
Washington, D.C.
Exhibition dates:
December 17, 1981–February 28, 1982

Photographic Credits
Unless otherwise noted,
photographs are courtesy of the lender.

Library of Congress Cataloging in Publication Data

Fox, Howard N.
Metaphor, new projects by contemporary sculptors, Hirshhorn Museum and Sculpture Garden.

Catalog of an exhibition held Dec. 17, 1981–Feb. 28, 1982.

1. Sculpture, American—Exhibitions.
2. Sculpture, Modern—20th century—United States—Exhibitions. 3. Metaphor in art—Exhibitions. 4. Conceptual art—United States—Exhibitions.
I. Hirshhorn Museum and Sculpture Garden. II. Title.
NB212.F68 709'.73'0740153
81-607122
AACR2

CONTENTS

FOREWORD

Traditionally art museums have been thought of as the storehouses of culture; indeed, museums, like libraries, have served the noble purpose of preserving the past for the future. In the last several years, however, museums of modern art have been called upon to participate in the culture of the living moment, not simply by exhibiting or collecting examples of contemporary art, as has long been their function, but by acting as a sort of midwife in the birth and destiny of innovative art. Now, in addition to its usual role, the museum has been challenged to assume the greater participatory role of a theater in which the tableaus of contemporary culture are staged. Modern art museums, recognizing that their changing functions in society parallel the changes affecting the art they are committed to preserve and encourage, have attempted to respond to the challenge of the new. *Metaphor: New Projects by Contemporary Sculptors,* which brings together for the first time six artists whose sculpture and artistic vision can be investigated as a significant direction in American art today, is just such a response.

Each of the six projects in this exhibition was conceived especially for this exhibition; none had existed previously, and it is altogether likely that at least some of them will never exist in quite the same form again. This suits the artists, who—like many of their colleagues working in site-specific, temporary, or large-scale installations—might not otherwise have had such an opportunity for want of an exhibition space or the necessary resources. For the museum, these endeavors must inevitably be approached with some trepidation, since its object is to select, or merely anticipate, projects for exhibition literally sight unseen. Museums of modern art must be willing to undertake this kind of risk, however, if they are to respond to the imperatives of contemporary art.

Of course, none of this denies the quality of aesthetic expression that may ultimately take form in the museum setting. The projects in this exhibition are sculptures first of all; they utilize many of the traditional expressive means available to the medium, asserting their forceful physical presence through scale, stylized design, manipulation of space, the exploitation of material properties, workmanship, and a not insignificant dose of sheer visual spectacle. Because they take the form of machines, architecture, or highly theatrical environments, these projects may not initially be perceived as the sculptural works that they are. Yet these inventions do tend to engage the viewer in ways that have become increasingly significant to many of the most inquiring of contemporary artists—ways that have not often been associated with modern sculpture. Rather than presenting themselves as discrete objects for passive observation, these projects may surround or engulf the viewer; some require the viewer's actual participation; some even perform an activity of their own at scheduled "performance" times.

Their sculptural and physical characteristics aside, these works (as the title of the exhibition implies) are also about ideas. Working *through* their physical form, each of these constructions conveys a dense and often difficult matrix of ideas for which the projects are metaphors and highly elaborated literary conceits, embodying their creators' visions of the individual, his place in society, the creative process, even the creation or destruction of the world. Given such complex and deep-seated subjects, it is hardly surprising that the projects themselves are complex. In that they both encourage and require individual interpretation to become a "complete" aesthetic experience for the viewer, they take their place within the traditional intellectual and emotional processes of the art experience.

These ambitious projects doubtless will puzzle many viewers; it is the continuing fate of contemporary art to be challenging and provocative. The Hirshhorn Museum's undertaking to produce an exhibition of these specially commissioned works represents a response in good faith to developments in contemporary art and an expression of our confidence that these six artists are outstanding representatives of the continuing search for new and expressive artistic directions.

Abram Lerner
Director

ACKNOWLEDGMENTS

Among the happiest aspects of preparing an exhibition catalog is the opportunity to thank the many individuals who have contributed to the realization of the exhibition. It is all the more gratifying in this instance, since organizing this exhibition has sometimes seemed as complex and unwieldy as the six specially commissioned projects that comprise it. Fortunately, *Metaphor: New Projects by Contemporary Sculptors* has benefited from the good offices of numerous professionals within and outside the Hirshhorn Museum whose support I wish to acknowledge.

My first thanks must go to Director Abram Lerner and Deputy Director Stephen E. Weil for their early and sustained support of this exhibition; their encouragement and benevolent concern, especially during some of its more hectic phases, are deeply appreciated. I also wish to express my gratitude to the late Mr. Joseph H. Hirshhorn and Mrs. Hirshhorn for their interest and encouragement during a critical early stage of the exhibition's genesis.

Nancy Foster Kirkpatrick, the Museum's Executive Officer, deserves special thanks for engineering the solutions to the many technical, logistical, and administrative matters that are the byproducts of working in a public institution. In a very tangible way, this exhibition owes its realization to her expert guidance.

The efforts of other Museum personnel were similarly essential to mounting this show. Chief of Exhibits and Design Joe Shannon and his staff, headed by Edward Schiesser, are virtually the heroes of this exhibition. Faced with unprecedented challenges, they brought off the coordination of these complex installations with their customary uncanny expertise. John Tennant and Lee Stallsworth photographed the projects, establishing a permanent record of these ephemeral works of art. Public Information Officer Sidney S. Lawrence III and his co-worker Carol Parsons handled the public affairs for the exhibition with characteristic flair and good cheer; it is always a pleasure to work with them. Librarian Anna Brooke, *fidei defensor,* prepared the artists' bibliographies that appear herein; her work was earlier assisted by the efforts of Museum Intern Theresa Barnes and by summer volunteer Terrence Eagleton. Their contribution to this catalog is considerable. And Penine Hart, herself a dandy of a word processor, prepared the catalog manuscript on an electronic apparatus that I should have thought was a part of the exhibition.

The nature of this exhibition, whose actual contents materialized only days before its public opening, required special accommodations by the Smithsonian Institution Press in order for a fully documented catalog to be made available while the installations were on display. I wish to thank Managing Editor Maureen Jacoby and Production Manager Lawrence J. Long for their indulgence in making this feasible. Carol Hare designed this handsome publication and John Harris has been a ready, willing, and very able editor; both of them have worked valiantly against tight deadlines and have my warmest thanks. I am especially happy to thank independent editor Carole Jacobs, whose tireless queries and deft red pen have coaxed this text into its present form. Her patient (and occasionally impatient) counsel, as well as the pleasure of her company, have been invaluable to me.

Most of all it is, of course, the artists (and their assistants) who must be credited for truly creating this exhibition. Their ideas and enthusiasm in planning and working with the Museum have made this project uniquely engaging. The merit of their work speaks for itself; the satisfaction of working with them is a felicity that is mine to speak, and I am very pleased indeed to have this occasion to do so.

H.N.F.

INTRODUCTION

A Modest Proposal

Deep within the Modernist tradition—that century-long quest for a nonobjective, reductively purified, absolute art which began with Impressionism and culminated in Minimal art—and secreted within the soul of its many clangorous revolutions, there exists a fundamental mistrust of art itself. It is a mistrust that dates back at least to Plato's judgment that in art, form and content are divisible and come together only in an imitation of Truth. Plato viewed the artifice and deception of art as being so removed from the Ideal forms it represents that he banished art from his hypothesized Republic. Happily, in this less than ideal world, art has persisted, albeit along with the heavy influence of Plato's demand for the revelation of absolute truth. In the modern world, his notions have given rise to a concept, or perhaps an attitude, about ideals and essences in art, and many Modernist artists and critics, themselves latter-day Platonists, have attempted to reconcile this understood dissociation between form and content. Until about the late 1960s, virtually every significant art movement of the twentieth century in some way addressed this problem.

The Modern aesthetic, articulated repeatedly through the twentieth century from Kasimir Malevich to Piet Mondrian to Brice Marden, has been a transcendental aesthetic—a belief in an ideal art of purity, autonomy, sublimity; a search for an art that would obey only its own laws and reveal its own ideal forms, eschewing all relation with the non-art world. Indeed, the "natural history" of Modernist art, through its many incarnations, has been one of evolution to a condition utterly divorced from all extraneous, "non-art" properties. Unquestionably, the most significant and revolutionary ideas of twentieth-century art have come in those nonobjective, abstract movements—Cubism, Suprematism, Abstract Expressionism, Minimalism, and similar formalist tendencies—that persisted and became the dominant movements which have formed our understanding of "modern" art and sensibility; other episodes—Symbolist-derived movements such as Fauvism, Expressionism, and Surrealism—have been somehow *un*-Modern, and decidedly sublunary by comparison. Unlike the formalist tendencies, wherein form and content were seen as one and the same, these Symbolist movements—in which form *implied* content—entailed no reconciliation of Plato's dissociation of object and idea; perhaps this is what was so un-Modern about them. By contrast, much very recent art, including the projects in this exhibition, is based on and derives its expressive power from this very rift.

The apparent diversity for which recent art is notorious may make postulation of *any* shared component seem extravagant. A thoughtful examination of the art itself and the tradition against which it was generated, however, indicates that an element of commonality in much of very recent art is both perceptible and logical.

The foundations and prestige of the Modernist sensibility began to erode quite noticeably in the 1960s, yielding to both the internal exhaustion of the tradition and the concomitant development of what often has been described as post-Modern art. This rubric has come to encompass the polytypical glut of work which gave rise to the commonplace that the art history of the 1970s, and now of the '80s, has been one of diversity, multiplicity, plural*ism*—as though such apparent fragmentation in the art scene somehow constituted an "ism." This perception of discontinuity has not always prevailed: the art of the twentieth century had tended to be read somewhat linearly, as a progression—however fitful and erratic—of essential styles, succeeding one another in ascendancy and decline. But with the last vestiges of that orderly succession dissipating—or at least with the hegemony of such a reading of art history giving out—in the late 1960s, the art scene seemed to become an aesthetic free-for-all.

Critical response to this heterogeneity has been far from unanimous. The critic Hilton Kramer, who has often spoken disparagingly of what he once called the "postmodern sweepstakes,"[1] recently reiterated his belief that "if there is something appealing in the very openness of this post modern scene, there is also something dismaying" in its reminder that "ours is now a culture without a focus or a center—a culture desperately engaged in ransacking the past, including the very recent past, in the hope of discovering an identity that can win our credence."[2] Wondering aloud whether we are "condemned . . . in the art of the '80s to remain in a perpetual whirl of countervailing and contradictory styles and attitudes," he concluded that the "eager embrace of art of every persuasion . . . satisfies our hearty new appetite for esthetic experience while requiring nothing from us in the way of commitment or belief."[3] In contrast, artist and commentator Douglas Davis has theorized that only "a figure vivid enough and powerful enough to focus our vision" on the state of our art and culture is required for comprehension of post-Modern diversity, suggesting as a possibility the image of "the fiber-optic cable, crammed with hundreds of filaments, each one carrying a television, telephone, or computer data signal, each one bearing a message all its own from sender to receiver. Each one running beside the others, discrete and together, inside this great cable that almost resembles the new, extraordinarily different, and unpredictable decade."[4] Davis clearly is not unsympathetic to Kramer's concerns, though his stance here as in all of his writings on the subject is much more enthusiastic and welcoming of the apparent panoply of post-Modern modalities.

A third school of thought posits that it is possible, perhaps necessary, to discern a single or integrated underlying impulse amid the thicket of recent styles and non-styles. The critic Rosalind Krauss has asked whether "the absence of a collective style [is] the token of a real difference? Or is there not something for which all these terms for contemporary art are possible manifestations?"[5] One need not agree or disagree with Krauss's findings about the "index" as a model that informs so much apparently diverse contemporary art or with her methodology of structuralist analysis to appreciate the rightness of her question and the value of its ramifications. She is correct, I think, in her presumption that, whatever the nature of the contemporary art scene, it is neither randomly mutant nor unamenable to analysis.

Any account of very recent art would have to acknowledge that there has been a decline of the Modernist aesthetic that vested such value in the facture of the art object and the way it looked. Thus, no patently stylistic account—*de facto* a formalistic one—could adequately explain this period, whose continuing evolution resists stylistic categorization and whose most ambitious work is not generated by formal concerns in the first place. What *does* characterize much of post-Modern three-dimensional art and distinguishes the oeuvres of some of the most advanced artists working today is an oblique approach to the delivery of content, a conceptual organization on *linguistic* models, particularly metaphor. For present purposes, metaphor simply denotes the presentation of one mode or system of reality in terms of another. Of course the functioning of metaphor is not simple; its theory, structure, and praxis are treated in depth by a vast body of literature. What is important here, however, is not a protracted analysis of metaphor but a consideration of its peculiar manifestations in contemporary art.[6]

It is justifiable, I feel, to propose that metaphor is the root of some of the most intelligent and problematic work by contemporary artists, six of whom are represented in this exhibition. Many others could have been chosen as deservedly, but the strong resonances among the work of these six establish a rather coherent focus. These resonances have little to do with style, stemming rather from the conceptual basis of the work and its presentation through the structure of metaphor. It is not these artists' recourse to content that is revolutionary or even especially noteworthy; content is as old as art. Nor is it any other "literary" mode, such as narrative or the combination of image with text, that is distinctive here. It is their use of linguistic *models,* or conceptual principles, in three-dimensional art that is so significant. Several of these artists and their thoughtful observers have acknowledged the linguistic basis of their art. Dennis Oppenheim has called his work "a kind of metalanguage"[7] and Lauren Ewing has referred to "language displacement" in hers.[8] Language has also been mentioned as Vito Acconci's "ubiquitous partner."[9]

It is as if these artists have discovered in language and its operations the most plastic and expressive medium of all. Their interest in metaphor seems, moreover, to have been a necessary consequence of the options available to them at the close of the Modernist tradition. That they should be using metaphor at all suggests a presumption that art need not describe (narcissistically) only itself and its qualities and, further, that the value of art—for artist and viewer alike—may not inhere in the object *per se.*

The use of linguistic models has enabled these artists and many others to produce a new art in which form and content often are disjunctive; a highly theatrical art that synthesizes different arts; a multivalent art that addresses itself not only to the eye, but to the mind's eye as well. It is, in its lofty ambitions, often a "difficult" art, but its operation and the components of that operation are comprehensible and worthy of closer scrutiny.

Synthesis and Disjunction

Modern art ended very much as it had begun, with the quest for an absolute art. Its history was a century-long process of fractional distillation, a quest to clarify and delimit the matrix of artistic concerns. Each of its movements has asserted itself as a modality apart from and indifferent to "natural" appearances and the objects of the daily world. Eventually, within the Modernist sensibility the virtuosity of the artist came to consist, as critic Clement Greenberg said, of rendering substance "entirely optical."[10] Greenberg argued that the Modern object, whether two- or three-dimensional, must be sufficient and self-sufficient, so that "every conceivable as well as perceptible element belongs altogether to the work of art [and] the positivist aspect of the modernist 'aesthetic' finds itself most fully realized."[11] The dialectical progression of Modernist art history ultimately decreed that the object itself be fractioned out (in conceptual art), at once restoring content and removing even the material barrier that interceded between the essence of art and its realization. Clearly, the art of the twentieth century that had defined its (increasingly restrictive) perimeters by the manipulation of forms and the way they appear had exhausted its potential for continued development. The *idea* of Modernism—which is not to say its handiworks or its prestige—had terminated.

Once this thoughtful and programmed dialectic had brought the reductive ideal to its limits, it seemed historically inevitable and indeed only logical that artists would be impelled to explore additive, synthesized forms. The eclectic results of this impulse are everywhere in evidence, from strains of decorative paintings in which multiple styles are juxtaposed in a single canvas, to three-dimensional objects which combine painterly and sculptural concerns at the same time, to video and performance art which manipulates space much as environmental sculpture does. Such combinative forms often are little more than cleverly reconstituted formalism, but even they partake of the general notion of synthesis. Other, more problematic, developments have involved performance art, site-specific environmental installations, temporal and ephemeral art forms, such immaterial manifestations as sound and light art, artistic collaborations, and other "intermedia" forms that all beg some alignment with the visual arts but freely combine them with poetry, theater, music, dance, architecture, cinema, video, etc. The pervasiveness of such synthetic new art forms seems a necessary reaction to the logical terminus of the Modern reductive ideal in Minimal art.

This synthesizing process has marked affinities with *collage,* an art form that has persisted throughout Modern art but which has always been relegated to a minor rank. It is not difficult to understand why. When collage is accepted as a Modern development it is usually explained as an experimental mixing of media—hence the wide use of the formalist term "mixed media" to describe collage. But this label is inadequate as a definition; reflecting the Modernist bias that favored fidelity to the "intrinsic" properties of materials, it describes the surface of the works rather than the true nature of collage. When it first appeared around 1912 in the Cubist experiments of Pablo Picasso and Georges Braque, collage was less a mixing of media than it was the superimposition of one mode of reality—that is, a *non-art* reality (in the form of newspaper clippings, simulated wood-grain papers, theater tickets, etc.)—into another mode of reality—an *art* reality. In collage an object such as a theater ticket may remain materially intact yet be *virtually* transformed within its alien context. Thus, collage embodies a *situational* aesthetic more than a material one. Collage, the concerns of which were incompatible with the Modern drive for "purely formal" art, was abandoned early on by its earliest pioneers; ever since, it has remained of only secondary interest to Modernism, which developed within formal rather than situational aesthetics. Yet it can be stated with reason that the synthesizing, situational aesthetic of collage has become the activating principle in the art of the last decade and shows every sign of continuing that role in the present one.

Contemporary art is characterized, furthermore, by a disjunctive mode that is co-functional with synthesis and the collage principle. Where Modern art came to approach as nearly as possible an ideal objecthood that would be manifest in "only one property," as Robert Morris once wrote of it,[12] post-Modern art allows—indeed seems to require—an art that is disjunctive in form and multivalent in meaning. In post-Modern art we find intricate and subtle ideas reflected in incongruous combinations, unresolved tensions, incompletely assimilated forms, and a tendency toward the presentation of the whole as a scheme of complex implied relationships of so many discrete, if interdependent, parts.

Synthesis and disjunction, then, are the two principle coordinates about which recent art evolves. Implicit in these modes is the urge toward metaphoric art, which, like collage, superimposes one system of reality on another with a resulting disjunction, or dissociation, of intended meaning from empirical form. The metaphoric mode issues logically and inevitably from the operation of synthesis and disjunction in contemporary art, and it is not too much to nominate it as the fullest and most literate development of contemporary art.

Theater and Theatricality: Setting the Stage

Theatre and theatricality are at war today, not simply with modernist painting (or modernist painting and sculpture), but with art as such—and to the extent that the different arts can be described as modernist, with modernist sensibility as such.

When Michael Fried wrote these words in 1967 in his widely read essay "Art and Objecthood,"[13] the authority of the Modernist sensibility to which he alluded was already becoming susceptible to the gathering foundations of a new sensibility, as he plainly recognized in his ominous warning. Fried cited sculptors such as Robert Morris (whose current metaphoric projects are radically different from the objects he was making in the mid-1960s), Donald Judd, and Tony Smith, all of whom had begun exploring the way in which environment, scale, placement, and repetition could influence the manner in which the most simplifed of their "minimal" or "primary" structures—cubes, cylinders, and other basic solids—were perceived. Despite the widespread impression that such forms were acausal, meaningless, and inert, their authors asserted that such works existed *necessarily in relation* to the environment and the viewer and were not the "autistic" objects they seemed. In fact, it was specifically because such "literalist art," as Michael Fried called it, was *not* self-sufficient and *was* affected by conditions external to its own materiality that he faulted it as being, in his word, *theatrical.* Literalist art, Fried argued, was anthropomorphic in scale, relational to human movement, placed so as to confront the viewer—to be "in his way." Its theatricality consisted in its "latent or hidden naturalism."

Whether the "literalist art" of the sculptors Fried cites broke with the Modern tradition (as both they and Fried claimed) or whether it represented an apotheosis of Modernism (as the extreme reduction and purity of the objects themselves suggest) is still open to debate.

Fried's criticism, however, addressed literalist art as a clear and present danger, misguided in its conception, banal in its results. *"The success, even the survival of the arts,"* he argued, *"has come increasingly to depend on their ability to defeat theatre."* Moreover, he asserted, *"Art degenerates as it approaches the condition of theatre,"* concluding that *"The concepts of quality and value—and to the extent that these are valuable to art, the concept of art itself—are meaningful, or wholly meaningful, only* within *the individual arts. What lies between the arts is theatre"* [Fried's italics throughout].

Fried's argument was so entrenched in the Modern vision that it was not necessary for him to explain exactly *why* art "degenerates" as it becomes theatrical or *how* quality and value inhere only within the individual, i.e., accepted, arts and their established divisions. Recognizing Fried's analysis as a major statement of its time, proffered as an implied standard for future art, one must question its applicability to the art that has followed it, emerging, as so much of it has, *between* the traditional media. Very recent art is so deliberately, essentially, and multifariously theatrical that Fried's focus on the confrontational and material aspects of theatricality in the visual arts is inadequate to deal with it.

A broader notion of theatricality seems to be required here. Theatricality may be considered as that propensity in the visual arts for a work to reveal itself within the mind of the beholder as something other than what it is known empirically to be. This is precisely antithetical to the Modern ideal of the wholly manifest, self-sufficient object; and theatricality may be the single most pervasive property of post-Modern art.

The projects in this exhibition are extravagantly theatrical in both presentation and concept. Certainly they lie between the traditional media, often within a single work combining sculpture, literature (texts, notations, inscriptions, etc.) and linguistic modes, architecture, and performative elements (particularly in such projects as Alice Aycock's or Dennis Oppenheim's constructions that actually move and do things). They are passively confrontational with the viewer in their basically human scale and in the overwhelming complexity which both requires them to be perceived in stages (by exploration, rather than all at once) and provokes but does not always satisfy the desire for comprehension. Some of them are actively confrontational, demanding for their completion the active participation of the "viewer," as do Vito Acconci's vehicular contraptions which require the viewer to actually pedal a bicycle or sit in a swing to precipitate a series of other events, or Siah Armajani's architectural constructions that serve as reading rooms or meeting places which are "complete" only with the presence of participants.

Beyond these salient intermedia and confrontational factors, which reflect Michael Fried's notion of theatricality, such projects are theatrical in the very manner of their presentation, which often includes elements of traditional stagecraft. For example, dramatic lighting serves this sort of work not only to illuminate and highlight the constructions but also to produce a nearly palpable environment, an effect created by Robert Morris, for instance, in a recent installation whose only light came from a series of eerily glowing cenotaphs placed around the perimeter of the space. Sound effects are sometimes used, as in certain of Lauren Ewing's architectural constructions in which electronic sensors respond to the presence of viewers by emitting sounds. And some constructions even "perform" activities at scheduled times, rapidly attracting an audience.

These works are clearly theatrical in the usual sense of the term; they exist not in and of themselves but rather are presented in and for a given circumstance. They are situational, participatory, and operational in "real" time and "real" space. They are exaggerated and unnatural presentations staged for an audience. But they are also theatrical in a more profound and essential sense; their very conceptual foundation in an operation of language is itself theatrical. Not all language is verbal, but all language—indeed all *organized* communication—is theater. Communication is metaphoric as well as theatrical in its basic operation: thought must be converted to symbols such as written words, spoken words, gestures, images, sounds, objects, or other signifiers, and then reconverted to thought in the minds of the audience through a process of linguistic transubstantiation. Communication itself, then, is a pantomime of notions, beliefs, associations, conjectures, errors. It is a process through which nothing in the world can be absolute or even literal in its import but must be understood only in the arbitrary, albeit theoretically agreed upon, assignation of imperfect, clumsy meanings.

The metaphoric works of this exhibition reflect such a view of language and its equation into knowing consciousness. They acknowledge the theatricality of metaphor, in which one reality is advanced as another, surrogate, reality; appropriately, these artworks communicate with all the guile and falsity of theater, and they make no attempt, as the art forms of Modernism did, to bridge the Platonic rift between object and idea, between form and content. Here theater and artifice are recognized as basic conditions of human awareness.

Deus ex Machina

When Francis Picabia reinvented nubile sexuality in the guise of a spark plug he was not making a statement about the ontology of automobile parts. His *Portrait d'une jeune fille Américaine dans l'état de nudité* is of course metaphorical not of spark plugs but of his stated subject. Yet Picabia's famous mechanomorphic portraits dating from 1915, even now retaining their wit and novelty, represent a timely response to the same machine age that a few years earlier had galvanized the Italian and Russian Futurists and, in 1936, would be satirized in Charles Chaplin's *Modern Times.* Throughout this century the machine has been explored as both a subject and an aesthetic in art, as demonstrated in the historic exhibition *The Machine as Seen at the End of the Mechanical Age,* held at the Museum of Modern Art in 1968. That exhibition surveyed machine-oriented art from such unlikely precedents as drawings for fifteenth-century flying machines and seventeenth-century robotic creatures, all the way to the latest in laser-generated forms. Curator Pontus Hulten's notion that the machine age was in its historical decline was suggested by a sort of postlude to the exhibition that featured experiments with new technologies. No longer was the idea of the machine as significant as the interest in new material and formal possibilities; this formally observed obsolescence of the machine reflected the customary Modernist affinity for material innovation as an end in itself.

Quite recently the machine, or its ghost, has reappeared in the work of a number of artists around the country who have rediscovered in its archaic image new expressive possibilities. As Janet Kardon has pointed out,[14] such artists as Vito Acconci, Alice Aycock, and Dennis Oppenheim at once follow and advance a tradition of modern art with what she has called their "machineworks." This tradition notwithstanding, it would be misleading to argue that these artists are particularly interested in the machine age or its correlative issues of automation, industrialization, dehumanization, and conformity. Their fundamental engagement is less with the influence of machines on modern times than it is with the "language," the morphology, of machines—how they function syntactically, systemically, one part to another—as a structural model for their art. The machine *per se* is a non-issue; for them, the structure of the machine has left the daily world and entered the repertoire of poetic images.

It is not only the machine whose morphology has been adopted as praxis for metaphorical and related art. Other immediately recognizable morphologies, especially of furniture, clothing, vehicles, and architectural forms, have also come into wholesale use in contemporary sculpture as increasing numbers of artists have turned to "working from the model"[15]—that is, from a known morphology—to produce works that cannot properly be described as either representational or formalist in essence but which explore and exploit the separation between the "signified" (what is represented) and the "signifier" (the actual object), almost as if the sculptures were *hypothetical* of other objects or other concepts.[16] Among the artists in this exhibition, Vito Acconci frequently has used the forms of vehicles, usually bicycles, to organize and actuate his constructions, while architectural vocabularies have figured prominently in the oeuvres of Alice Aycock, Lauren Ewing, Siah Armajani, and Vito Acconci, as well as literally scores of other well-known and not-so-well-known artists. Yet this nearly rampant development of such architectural sculpture in the past decade has occurred virtually without precedent: until the 1970s there was certainly no *tradition* of architectural morphology providing the formal basis for sculpture.[17] The handful of instances that can be found (in the work of Alberto Giacometti or Isamu Noguchi, for example) are never cited as influences by the makers of this newer work. That this widespread preoccupation with architectural form should have happened at all, moreover without precedent, suggests that "machineworks," like the architectural sculpture to which they are so closely related, do not so much *continue* a Modern tradition[18] as establish a new and authentic modality that in fact may have begun a different, post-Modern, tradition.

Pleasures of the Text

How can it be determined that these constructions are artifice and not simply errant architecture or impossibly bollixed machines? And, if they are artifice, how are they distinguished as metaphor and not merely somebody's baroque caprice? The question is, in essence, how do these machines and vehicles and theaters demand to be taken seriously?

Like any operation of language, metaphor presumes the auditor to have some recognition of its component parts; if there is no recognition then virtually there is no metaphor, but only a miscellany of elements. Metaphor also presumes a systemic order or relationship superinduced on its elements, yet such an order must have, by definition, some aspect of falsity about it. Metaphor is understood to be not a statement of equivalence but a comparison of unlike parts which evokes a matrix of implied parallels; the significance of the parallels can be discerned only when some known subject is inflected as some other known subject that it decidedly is not (as in the exemplary case cited as a convenience in many discussions, Plautus's metaphor "Man is a wolf"). Perceptually, metaphor is construed to be only *partly* true and plausible as a comparison to some indeterminate degree (as the conjecture implied that the behavior of man may in some ways be like the behavior of a wolf). Thus, recognition and falsity—pretense, in essence—are necessary conditions of metaphoric structure. And metaphoric structure may accurately be described, like the post-Modern art which it informs, as synthetic, disjunctive, and theatrical.

In works by the artists in this exhibition, the necessary detection of their metaphorical nature occurs variously: it may be induced by *cues* discerned in the work itself; or through information supplied by titles, texts, or other *appendices* to the work; or through a knowledge of the context in which the work is presented. By whatever combination of means, a "textuality" or frame of reference by which to "read" these works must be generated to permit recognition of both their metaphorical nature and their specific content.

These works usually provide cues in the form of the familiar or recognizable objects and structures—such as bicycles in Acconci's projects, skeletons in Morris's, or conveyor belts and crankshafts in Oppenheim's—from which they are assembled. The cue comes in the simple suspension or subversion of the conventional use of these objects: obviously neither an Acconci bicycle placed in a gallery situation and harnassed to a surrounding structure nor an Acconci house made of flags is meant to function as or even to represent "real" bicycles or "real" houses; similarly, a cadre of black-painted or silver-leafed human skeletons hovering around the gallery ceiling or peeking out of black felt drapery at models of the earth neither serve their natural function as skeletons nor assume their normal "role" as remains; neither does Oppenheim's conveyor belt deliver any material product. In these examples we must conclude that since the flags and bones and crankshafts do not describe themselves, they must describe something else. Thus they become active as metaphoric elements. Likewise, Armajani's early bridges that connect no *particular* points, Ewing's diminutive asylums and mills, and Aycock's machines for catching ghosts neither perform their indicated functions nor are intended to, and so must be considered hypothetical bridges and asylums and machines whose "function" (or dysfunction) is defined by something else. Hence these structures effectively announce themselves as metaphorical.

Once this metaphor-related disordering (analogous to the falsity of verbal metaphor) is perceived, an additional "textuality" by which these works are encoded as metaphor may be imposed through titles and supplemental texts that function as an index to their content. Titles indicate the direction which the interpretation or exegesis of a given work may take: when Aycock, for example, announces a series of projects under the general title *The Machine That Makes the World,* she confers upon the works not a concrete identity but rather the potential for the extrapolation of meaning from the ill-defined contraptions that heave and sprawl through the gallery space. Titles of Oppenheim's works are equally suggestive and equally cryptic; a multi-part title such as *A Way Station for Launching an Obsolete Power. (A Thought Collision Factory in Pursuit of Journey). (Clip in a Rifle—A Weapon)* attests to the multivalent nature of the apparatus and suggests that variant "readings" of the project are in order.

Sometimes, longer pieces of prose accompany these jerry-built descriptive titles. Oppenheim's *Final Stroke—Project for a Glass Factory* includes—in addition to an extravaganza of chutes and hoppers, pulleys, a smokestack, a heater, a vacuum machine, and numerous glass panels—a lengthy prose-poem describing, in erotic language reminiscent of the love poems of John Donne, the "mating" of two imaginations through the anatomy of the machine. Similarly, Aycock has published extended poetical commentaries for many of her projects, just as Marcel Duchamp published elaborate annotations, called *The Green Box,* to his most enigmatic and complex work, *The Bride Stripped Bare by Her Bachelors, Even* [*The Large Glass*] (1915–23)—a metaphorical work that he realized in a polyphony of manifestations and substitute forms throughout his oeuvre.

While written text perhaps figures most prominently in the work of Aycock and Oppenheim, the other artists included in this exhibition use text and language in their work as well. Robert Morris's *Preludes (For A.B.)* (1980)—the first of the metaphorical projects that contrast so dramatically with his previous work—consisted of a sequence of cenotaphs, slabs of back-lit translucent Italian onyx, each bearing a text for victims of death by various causes. Displayed in relative darkness, these macabre texts glowed softly, creating a virtual atmosphere of words. Vito Acconci's earlist artistic pursuits, in the mid-1960s, were in poetry, and his poems were well-known through the network of small presses that today remain a major forum for serious literary activity. Acconci's early performance pieces, although they took him into a new art form, evolved out of his poetry, substituting the spoken for the written word. His recent house- and vehicle-like projects also are products of language and ideation. Siah Armajani's meeting or reading gardens are inscribed with statements on beauty and art by such American philosophers as John Dewey and Ralph Waldo Emerson, as though the spare, Shaker-like rooms and enclosures that form these "gardens" had been built as hallowed places in which to confront these lessons. Lauren Ewing also inscribes her architectural sculptures with words, phrases, or sentences, and sometimes includes video or audio programs which project almost incantatory streams of words or word pairs integral to the metaphorical content of her work. And although Ewing's black constructions always maintain their sculptural presence, they serve as readily to present, like slates, the written word.

Such texts impose a context, a frame of reference, a catalog of associations about these difficult-to-decipher works. The use of text brings into play an additional dimension of theatricality, removing these works even further from traditional, discrete media than they otherwise might be. As they transcend our notions of objects or even situations, they are metamorphosed, quite literally, into instruments of thought. Without losing their evocative power, they become more indefinite and unspecific than objects can be. The meaning of these thought-machines and houses and theaters is endless, and their locus is as much in what Robert Morris often has spoken of as "mental space" as it is in real space. These are perfect machines; even when they are static, they are in perpetual motion.

Given: 1. The Waterfall, 2. The Illuminating Gas —More on Duchamp

To have mentioned Marcel Duchamp as the most obvious modern predecessor of the artists in this exhibition in his use and publication of the text to his works underrates his deeper contribution to the development of recent metaphorical art. Although it would be inaccurate to cite him as an "influence" on these artists in the sense that a mentor "influences" his students or his disciples, he figures as a pioneering presence through an otherwise alien Modernist era. His example is detectible in the work of Acconci and Oppenheim and that of Aycock, who in her 1981 project at Philadelphia's Institute of Contemporary Art overtly acknowledged her debt to Duchamp with spiraling and rotary forms that unmistakably echoed similar forms in his *The Bride Stripped Bare by Her Bachelors, Even* [*The Large Glass*], housed just blocks away at the Philadelphia Museum of Art. In that same ICA exhibition, *Machineworks,* Dennis Oppenheim built a thought-exchange machine that invites comparison with the "bachelor apparatus" from Duchamp's work.

But contemporary metaphorical artists' most essential inheritance from Duchamp, significant beyond his imagery, beyond his use of text, beyond even his kindred spirit, is a structural model—that is, a *conceptual* principle—for the organization of their work. Duchamp was well-known for his disparagment of what he called "retinal art," a term that could apply to any of the Modernist movements committed to an essentially formalist aesthetic. Duchamp always sought something that the object could not disclose by itself. Nearly every mature work by Duchamp is to some extent metaphorical or ironic, and disjunctive in that it calls for knowledge or recognition of both the object and the ambient context outside of the object to make it complete as a statement. Its meaning emerges in the reading of a "given"—the object—through the filter of a context that transforms the object to "read" as something other than what it is known to be. In its simplest operation, this transformation is exhibited in Duchamp's most scandalous work, the coyly titled *Fountain.* In its original context, the object was a urinal. The alteration of its physical context alone transformed it. Contrary to a more jaundiced view, Duchamp was neither claiming that "it's art because I, as an artist, say it's art" nor perpetrating an arrogant practical joke. His "content" lay in the gesture rather than the object *per se;* the significance was that a change of context elicits a different response from the viewer, whose recognition of the anomaly completes the *Fountain* as a work of art.

Duchamp's introduction of the urinal into an art context was not equivalent to Edward Weston's photographing a toilet in order to reveal its abstract form. Weston's abstracting of the form may momentarily deceive the viewer (as often happens in his pictures), but even in the absence of recognition, the essentially formal aesthetic of Weston's imagery is apprehensible to the eye. It remains retinal art for all to see. By contrast, the import of Duchamp's *Fountain* would have been lost to any beholder who did not recognize the *specific* and *subverted* use of the fixture. (It is conceivable that some women in Duchamp's audience, never having seen the inside of a men's room, even in movies or photographs, may not have at first appreciated Duchamp's irony.)

A more complex example of metamorphosis-by-context is Duchamp's *Given: 1. The Waterfall, 2. The Illuminating Gas,* permanently installed at the Philadelphia Museum of Art. The work consists of a tableau concealed in a small room and visible only through a peephole in the door that reveals a nude in a grotesque landscape, illuminated by a Bec Auer-type gas lamp. The selectively juxtaposed "givens" of this project startle its viewers, engaging intellectual as well as visual attention. Duchamp's success in this regard is documented by the considerable body of speculative criticism directed to it in the past decade. And, like any art—especially metaphorical art—it is potentially enriched by the interpretations it stimulates.

The projects in this exhibition have more in common with the mysterious *Given: 1. The Waterfall, 2. The Illuminating Gas* than with Readymades such as the *Fountain.* Indeed, they are some of the most deliberate and intricate works imaginable. Unlike the Dadaist "rape" of the object, exemplified in the violated *Fur-Covered Cup, Saucer, and Spoon* (1936) by Meret Oppenheim, a "factory" by Dennis Oppenheim (no relation to Meret) evinces a subverted but *redeemed* usage of its constituent parts. The self-evident hilarity of Dadaist humor is basically unsuitable to the much more serious-minded, though not necessarily humorless, intention of the artists in this exhibition and others who share their concerns. Like Duchamp's most complex works, such as *The Large Glass* and its voluminous series of notes, these metaphorical works are enriched by annotation of almost any sort and, however opaque their meaning, they quite affirmatively *invite* interpretation. The viewer is engaged to bring—is engaged to *desire* to bring—all cognitive powers to the work; the viewer is engaged to reinvent the work in a reprise of the creative process.

The Subjects of the Artist

It seems ironic that these artists construct such unwieldy, elephantine contraptions, jerry-built architecture, and cartoonlike vehicles to evoke essentially cerebral and spiritual concerns that may have little to do with the material world. The "truths" that these constructions refer to and comment upon are not the reflexive, object-bound issues of their own material and formal properties but rather are imaginative metaphors that often require recourse to considerations beyond the realm of objects. Dennis Oppenheim, for example, enlists the morphology of the machine as a metaphor for the thought process; Vito Acconci's vehicles and mobile homes are deployed to raise issues of political conscience; Robert Morris's cenotaphs, soaring skeletons, and networks of tubes, lights, and mirrors are bound up with the artist's idea of self and may also offer a critique of contemporary society; Alice Aycock's wood or high-tech constructions stand for states of imagined madness and visions of the forces of creation; Lauren Ewing's black sheds, powerhouses, and asylums are ruminations on the nature of consciousness incarcerated by the body and society; and even Siah Armajani's quasi-utilitarian architecture does not serve as housing for physical activity or shelter for creature comforts, but rather provides a setting, an empty place, for the highest pursuits of the mind—communion, reading, meditation. For each of these artists, the subject is the mind, presented metaphorically.

The challenge of communicating within these themes, in any medium, is a heroic one calling for a profound and original response. The subtlety, complexity, and metaphysical focus which they share preclude literal treatment; by their very nature, the subjects of these six artists demand metaphorical manifestation.

Apologia pro Vita Sua

His cogitative faculties immersed
In cogibundity of cogitation . . .
—Henry Carey, *Chrononhotonthologos,* 1734

It is not surprising that the complex and elusive subjects dealt with by these artists manifest themselves in complex and elusive projects. Some viewers find anomalous works such as these off-putting; they may suspect variously that the artists are indulging in empty spectacle, that the works themselves are predicated upon arcane learning, or that the demands on their cognitive faculties are simply inappropriate. In fact, the problem is much more likely to be a lack of understanding of the metaphorical functioning of this art.

Like more conventional art, these works are meant to appeal most immediately to the senses. Their commanding presence, intricate construction, confrontational scale, striking subversion of the uses of familiar objects, and inclusion of the techniques of stagecraft—in a word, their theatricality—engage the viewer's attention visually and experientially, in space and in time. Beyond this superficial contact, however, the six artists exhibited here undertake to engage the viewer intellectually, to stimulate the imaginative deciphering of the complex of unlikely juxtapositions, disjunctive fabrications, and narrative annotations wherein lies the content of these works. In metaphoric art, what arrests the eye is to be interpreted by the mind.

It must be acknowledged, though, that interpretation and comprehensibility are a fundamental problem in metaphorical art, for we have on the one hand the immediacy of these stunning, often overwhelming constructions that are experienced in "the present tense" and on the other the activity of interpretation that explains and justifies these pieces retrospectively. It seems to be the very destiny of such works to play out that dissociation of form and content about which Plato, and most Modern artists, had such misgivings.

Beyond this basic difficulty, the equation of the "success" of this art with the interpretive process places extraordinary burdens on artists and viewers alike. Independent of the kind of essential ambiguity which allows richness and nuance within metaphor, there always exists a possibility that any specific metaphoric communication can somehow emerge skewed or utterly unrecognizable as a metaphor. The literature of the subject refers repeatedly to false, dead, dormant, and extinct metaphors, all rendered inoperative because the absence of "textuality" deprives them of their meaningfulness.

Approaching this art in full knowledge that it may function obliquely and without a precise one-to-one metaphorical relationship between image and content seems necessary and desirable to its appreciation and interpretation; it is appropriate to the nature of the work. However, some viewers are resistant to the very notion that interpretation rightly can be part of an art experience.

The reticence with which many people react to the idea of having to read something or decode visual cues as part of the assimilation of a work of art is both puzzling and disconcerting. What puzzles is that it is somehow much more pervasive a phenomenon in the visual arts than in the other arts. No one would presume, for example, that the exercise of mere literacy is sufficient to a full appreciation of Shakespeare; rereading of a play and some ruminative process are anticipated without complaint. Viewers' reluctance to approach art with more than visual receptivity is disconcerting in that it does not derive from viewer laziness or indifference but seems to be engendered, at least indirectly, by an attitude implicit in the Modernist aesthetic that somehow a work of art is wholly manifest visibly and is apprehensible all at once—an attitude that seems to suggest that you can and *ought to* "get it" all at once and optically. This attitude precludes the fuller, more complex, and multivalent response—which *cannot* be gotten immediately and comprehensively—that this metaphoric art is intended to evoke.

The argument that art which is primarily visual ought to communicate itself exclusively on an optical level seems to represent an artificial and unwelcome severance of the optic nerve from what lies beyond, and is not more persuasive than an argument for a visual art form that is heavy in ideational content. Certainly these projects and metaphorical artworks in general make their ultimate appeal to the intellect. This characteristic, along with the indeterminacy and mystery associated with these works, has led some interested viewers to question whether such projects as these even qualify as visual art—an inquiry that itself reflects an antiquated Modernist outlook on the divisions between the arts. The question, I think, is not whether these works are visual art—indeed, they are extravagantly visual works of art; the question is whether they are something *in addition to* visual art.

Clearly they are. In their appeal to the intellect these projects decidedly are *more* than primarily visual forms, and they likewise transcend their roles as powerful physical presences in a gallery setting. It is possible that the cognitive import of such works may be beyond interpretation to many viewers, but this is a risk the artists have demonstrated their willingness to take.

These projects and others like them require a different *kind* of attention from that which habitually has been accorded the visual art of the Modernist epoch. That they demand an acuity over and beyond visual acuity is perhaps the one characteristic of these works that is self-evident; the rest must be discerned patiently and deliberately, and often without any guaranty of certitude. Full appreciation of this art is a function of good faith, not of a "good eye." If this act of faith is withheld—that is, if these works are viewed as retinal events or even as amusing but absurd contraptions—then their metaphoric essence is missed and they look only like Dadaist objects that insult the aspirations of Modernist culture, which these works do not do; they depart from it.

An Immodest Proposal

The mission upon which these artists are embarking in their departure from Modernism is very deliberate and courageous, I think, no less so than the revolutions of the French Cubists or the Russian Futurists, even if nowadays such significant change is assimilated into an omnivorous art culture as energetically as those earlier challenges were resisted.

If there is something revolutionary about these metaphorical productions, it is not their synthetic nature or their high theatricality or their orientation to content. It is, rather, their confrontation of the inabsolute—indeed, very arbitrary—nature of art and objecthood, which are now acknowledged to be so subject to the vicissitudes of time, place, and viewer. It is also in their predication upon the altered relationships among artist and object and viewer. These new relationships deed considerable proprietary responsibility to the viewer, who is called upon not as a mere spectator but rather as an active participant in the establishment of meaningfulness, thus shifting the emphasis from objective form to its informing context. Finally, these projects are new in their use of non-visual models—linguistic ones, specifically—in work which otherwise aligns itself with the sculptural tradition in the visual arts; this surely is very un-Modern. More specifically, what renders these projects some of the most ambitious artistic expressions of our time is the metaphoric mode which both fulfills and inspires a certain grandeur of artistic vision nearly epic in scope—a vision in which the self-limiting issues of the object and its facture are subsumed to much larger and more humanistic concerns ranging from the inner life of the mind to the creation of the celestial universe. For these artists, an art form that sustained anything less would be an abrogation of their vision.

Notes

1. Hilton Kramer, "Art: 'Illustration and Allegory' on View," *New York Times,* May 23, 1980, sec. 3, p. 21.

2. Hilton Kramer, "Today's Avant-Garde Artists Have Lost the Power to Shock," *New York Times,* November 16, 1980, sec. 2, p. 27.

3. Ibid.

4. Douglas Davis, "Post Post-Art: Where Do We Go from Here?", *Village Voice,* June 25, 1979, p. 39.

5. Rosalind Krauss, "Notes on the Index: Seventies Art in America," *October* 3 (Spring 1977): 68.

6. Many interpretations of metaphor and of metaphoric structures such as allegory are applicable to a study of post-Modern art. Craig Owens's proposal that allegory is the essential structure of post-Modern art is particularly illuminating in this regard; see his "The Allegorical Impulse: Toward a Theory of Postmodernism," *October* 12 (Spring 1980): 67–86. The term "allegory" is both a generic and a structural term; I have preferred the more general "metaphor," which embraces allegory and applies to a broader range of symbolic art as well.

7. Conversation with the artist, January 9, 1981.

8. From an unpublished manuscript by Ewing entitled "Project Description for Skidmore College: *The Library,*" 1981.

9. Janet Kardon, "Metaphorical Machinery," in *Machineworks: Vito Acconci, Alice Aycock, Dennis Oppenheim,* exhibition catalog (Philadelphia: Institute of Contemporary Art, University of Pennsylvania, 1981), p. 9.

10. Clement Greenberg, "The New Sculpture," in his *Art and Culture* (Boston: Beacon Press, 1961), p. 144.

11. Ibid., p. 145.

12. Robert Morris, "Notes on Sculpture," Part 1, *Artforum* 4 (February 1966): 44. Morris acknowledged that such an object could not exist, "since nothing exists that has only one property," but explained that Modern art had raised the question of whether such an object *could* exist.

13. Michael Fried, "Art and Objecthood," *Artforum* 5 (Summer 1967): 12–23. Reprinted in Gregory Battcock, ed., *Minimal Art: A Critical Anthology* (New York: E. P. Dutton & Co., 1968), pp. 116–47. This and subsequent citations to Fried are to this text.

14. "Metaphorical Machines," in *Machineworks,* exhibition catalog (Philadelphia: Institute of Contemporary Art, University of Pennsylvania, 1981), pp. 6–15.

15. I am indebted to my colleague Phyllis Rosenzweig for this ironically descriptive phrase.

16. Scott Burton's tables and chairs, for example, are not merely furniture so highly "stylized" that they somehow are "fine" art rather than applied design (although it is certainly *possible* to interpret them as such), but instead vacillate between pure forms and their perceived roles as utilitarian objects, eluding either definition, suggesting themselves as "ideal," "platonic" *concepts* of tables or chairs. In this they are related to (but *only* related to, and not examples of) metaphorical art, whose import similarly shifts between signifier and signified.

17. Architectural *motifs* have long been used in decorative art and in certain traditions of funerary art. The closest that architectural form comes to being a foundation for any tradition of sculpture in Western art is in the eighteenth-century English garden follies built in the form of ruins, but there is no basis to suggest that these represent a source for architectural sculpture of the 1970s.

18. It must also be concluded that the relationship of metaphorical art to Dada is similarly limited, lacking the quotient of anarchy, nihilism, and social affront characteristic of Dada antics. In fact this work has closer affinities with the highly metaphoric art of Surrealism, although it lacks the subrational and subconscious "appeal" elemental to Surrealist art and ideology.

CATALOG

This catalog is arranged alphabetically by artist. Each artist's section includes professional biographical information, a selected bibliography, and a brief survey of representative previous works, as well as photographs and commentary.

Dimensions, which are approximate, are given in meters (and feet), height x width x depth.

Project installations in this exhibition have been photographed by John Tennant and Lee Stallsworth. Photographs of other works are individually credited in the catalog.

Vito Acconci

Born in Bronx, New York, January 24, 1940.
Lives in Brooklyn, New York.

Education

B.A., Holy Cross College, Worcester, Massachusetts, 1962.
M.F.A., University of Iowa, Iowa City, 1964.

Awards

National Endowment for the Arts Artists Fellowship, 1976, 1978.

John Simon Guggenheim Memorial Foundation Fellowship, 1979.

Selected Solo Exhibitions

Rhode Island School of Design, Providence, 1969.

Gain Ground Gallery, New York, 1970.

Nova Scotia College of Art and Design, Halifax, 1970.

A Space, Toronto, 1971.

Protetch-Rivkin Gallery, Washington, D.C., 1971.

John Gibson Gallery, New York, 1971.

Sonnabend Gallery, New York, and Galerie Ileana Sonnabend, Paris, 1972–79.

California Institute of the Arts, Valencia, 1972.

Galeria D, Brussels, 1973, 1977.

Portland (Oregon) Center for the Visual Arts, 1975.

Museum of Conceptual Art, San Francisco, 1975.

Hallwalls, Buffalo, 1975.

The Kitchen Center for Video, Music and Dance, New York, 1976, 1978, 1980, 1981.

Wright State University, Dayton, Ohio, 1976.

Anthology Film Archives, New York, 1976, 1977.

The Clocktower, Institute for Art and Urban Resources, New York, 1977.

Centre d'Art Contemporain, Geneva, 1977.

Galleria Salvatore Ala, Milan, 1978.

San Francisco Museum of Modern Art, 1978.

International Cultureel Centrum, Antwerp, 1978.

Stedelijk Museum, Amsterdam, 1978.

Young Hoffman Gallery, Chicago, 1979, 1981.

Museum of Contemporary Art, Chicago, 1980.

Atlanta Art Workers Coalition, 1980.

Max Protetch Gallery, New York, 1981.

Selected Group Exhibitions

Language 3, Dwan Gallery, New York, 1969.

Software, The Jewish Museum, New York, 1970.

Information, The Museum of Modern Art, New York, 1970.

Body Art, John Gibson Gallery, New York, 1971.

7e Biennale de Paris, 1971.

Documenta V, Kassel, West Germany, 1972.

American Drawings 1963–1973, Whitney Museum of American Art, New York, 1973.

72nd American Exhibition, Art Institute of Chicago, 1976.

Eight Contemporary Artists, The Museum of Modern Art, New York, 1974.

Instant House, 1980
Installation at The Kitchen Center for Video, Music, and Dance, New York
Flags, pulley system, swing, wooden frames
2.5 × 6.4 × 6.4 (8 × 21 × 21)

Self-erecting room, or house, activated by a swing.

In the initial (unactivated) phase, four American flags—wall-size and attached to wooden frames—lie on the floor in a cross-shape around a central wooden framework: there are cuts in three of the flags (at this stage, as the flags lie undefined on the floor, the cuts are probably noticeable but not readable, they are seen simply as cuts, without a function).

In the middle of the central framework, in the middle of the flags, a swing hangs down from the ceiling (in the first installation, the swing was made of metal, like a conventional playground swing, in the second installation the swing was made of wood, like the framework of the other parts): the walls are connected by rope to a pulley-system that holds the swing.

When a person sits down on the swing, the swing descends to the floor, the flags rise up around the swing and become the walls of a room, a house: the cuts are definable now as door and windows (or eyes and ears and mouth or nose); inside the house—the part available to the participant—the walls are the American flags that have been spread out on the floor; outside the house—the part available to the public—the walls are what had been the unseen underside of the American flags, the walls are Russian flags.

—Vito Acconci

Bodyworks, Museum of Contemporary Art, Chicago, 1975.

Video Art, Institute of Contemporary Art, University of Pennsylvania, Philadelphia, 1975.

Venice Biennale, 1976, 1978, 1980.

Language and Structure in North America, Kensington Art Center, Toronto, 1976.

Biennial Exhibition, Whitney Museum of American Art, New York, 1977, 1981.

Improbable Furniture, Institute of Contemporary Art, University of Pennsylvania, Philadelphia, 1977.

Time, Philadelphia College of Art, 1977.

Journées interdisciplinaires sur l'art corporel et les performances, Centre Georges Pompidou, Paris, 1978.

Concept, Narrative, Document, Museum of Contemporary Art, Chicago, 1979.

Sound, P.S. 1, Institute for Art and Urban Resources, New York, 1979.

Morris, Acconci, Oppenheim, Sonnabend Gallery, New York, 1980.

Machineworks: Vito Acconci, Alice Aycock, Dennis Oppenheim, Institute of Contemporary Art, University of Pennsylvania, Philadelphia, 1981.

Westkunst: Zeitgenössische Kunst seit 1939, Museen der Stadt Köln, West Germany, 1981.

Other Realities: Installations for Performance, Contemporary Arts Museum, Houston, 1981.

Selected Bibliography

Acconci, Vito. *Avalanche,* no. 6 (Fall 1972; special Acconci issue): 2–80.

———."Excerpts from 'Other Voices for a Second Sight.' " In *Individuals: Post-Movement Art in America,* edited by Alan Sondheim, pp. 26–67. New York: E. P. Dutton and Co., 1977.

———. "Notebook: Vito Acconci on Activity and Performance." *Art and Artists* 6 (May 1971): 68–69.

———. "Plot." *Tracks* 2 (Spring 1976): 8–22.

———. "Towards a Theory of Image/Instrument/Decoration." *Cover* 2 (January 1980): 22–25.

Avgikos, Jan. "Interview: Vito Acconci." *Art Papers* 5 (January–February 1981): 1–5.

Béar, Liza. "Vito Acconci . . . Command Performance." *Avalanche Newspaper,* May–June 1974, pp. 21–23.

Borden, Lizzie. "Cosmologies." *Artforum* 11 (October 1972): 45–50.

———. "Directions in Video Art." In *Video Art,* exhibition catalog, pp. 75–89. Philadelphia: Institute of Contemporary Art, University of Pennsylvania, 1975.

Burnham, Jack. "Acconci in a Tight Spot." *New Art Examiner* 7 (May 1980): 1, 8–9.

———. "Interview [with Acconci], March 21, 1980." *New Art Examiner* 7 (May 1980): 1, 10–11.

Celant, Germano. "Vito Acconci." *Domus* 509 (April 1972): 54–56.

Davis, Douglas. *Artculture: Essays on the Post-Modern.* New York: Harper and Row Publishers, 1977.

Diacono, Mario. *Vito Acconci: Dal testo—azione al corpo come testo.* New York: Out of London Press, 1975.

Dickie, George. "What is Anti-Art?" *Journal of Aesthetics and Art Criticism* 33 (Summer 1975): 419–21.

Glozer, Laszlo. *Westkunst: Zeitgenössische Kunst seit 1939,* exhibition catalog. Cologne: DuMont Buchverlag, 1981.

Goldberg, RoseLee. *Performance: Live Art 1909 to the Present,* pp. 100–101. New York: Harry N. Abrams, 1979.

Henri, Adrian. *Total Art: Environments, Happenings, and Performance.* New York: Praeger Publishers, 1974.

Herman, Jerry. "Arts Reviews: 3 Installations: Sonnabend." *Arts Magazine* 54 (June 1980): 33–34.

Jordan, James. "A Critic Reveal(ed)(ing)." *Dialogue,* November–December 1980, pp. 4–5.

Kardon, Janet. *Time,* exhibition catalog, pp. 34–35. Philadelphia: Philadelphia College of Art, 1977.

Kirshner, Judith Russi. *Vito Acconci: A Retrospective, 1969 to 1980,* exhibition catalog. Chicago: Museum of Contemporary Art, 1980.

Kozloff, Max. "Pygmalion Reversed." *Artforum* 14 (November 1975): 30–37.

Krauss, Rosalind. "Notes on the Index: Seventies Art in America." *October* 3 (Spring 1977): 68–81.

Kurtz, Bruce. "Documenta 5: A Critical Preview." *Arts Magazine* 46 (Summer 1972): 30–43.

Larson, Kay. "Metaphysical Attraction." *Village Voice,* March 17, 1980, p. 79.

Sliding Doorway, 1981
Installation at the Whitney Museum of American Art, New York
Bicycle, black lace, camouflage netting, gold and silver painted wood, photo-mural wallpaper, pulley system
2.5 × 2.6 × 8.5 (8 × 8½ × 28)

Levine, Edward. "In Pursuit of Acconci." *Artforum* 15 (April 1977): 38–41.

———. "Vito Acconci." *Arts Magazine* 51 (January 1977): 6.

Lippard, Lucy R. *Six Years: The Dematerialization of the Art Object from 1966 to 1972.* New York: Praeger Publishers, 1973.

Machineworks: Vito Acconci, Alice Aycock, Dennis Oppenheim, exhibition catalog. Philadelphia: Institute of Contemporary Art, University of Pennsylvania, 1981.

McShine, Kynaston, L., ed. *Information,* exhibition catalog. New York: The Museum of Modern Art, 1970.

Mayer, Rosemary. "Performance and Experience." *Arts Magazine* 47 (December 1972): 33–36

Morgan, Stuart. "Reviews: Philadelphia: 'Machineworks, Institute of Contemporary Art.' " *Artforum* 19 (Summer 1981): 97–98.

Morris, Robert. "Aligned with Nazca." *Artforum* 14 (October 1975): 26–39.

———. "Some Splashes in the Ebb Tide." *Artforum* 11 (February 1973): 42–49.

Nemser, Cindy. "An Interview with Vito Acconci." *Arts Magazine* 45 (March 1971): 20–23.

Pincus-Witten, Robert. "Theatre of the Conceptual: Autobiography and Myth." *Artforum* 12 (October 1973): 40–46.

———. "Vito Acconci and the Conceptual Performance." *Artforum* 10 (April 1972): 47–49.

Raynor, Vivien. "Art: Noise in the Attic from Vito Acconci." *New York Times,* December 9, 1977, sec. C, p. 19.

Rickey, Carrie. "Vito Acconci: The Body Impolitic." *Art in America* 68 (October 1980): 118–23.

Rooms P.S.1, exhibition catalog, pp. 100–101. New York: Institute for Art and Urban Resources, 1977.

Salle, David. "Vito Acconci's Recent Work." *Arts Magazine* 51 (December 1976): 90–91.

Sass, Ann. "The Elusive Self: Metaphor and Metonymy in the Work of Vito Acconci." In *Fourth Annual Goodson Symposium on American Art,* unpaginated. New York: Whitney Museum of American Art, 1981.

Schwartz, Ellen. "Vito Acconci: 'I Want to Put the Viewer on Shaky Ground.' " *Art News* 80 (Summer 1981): 93–99.

Sharp, Willoughby. "Body Works." *Avalanche* 1 (Fall 1970): 14–17.

Skoggard, Ross. "Vito Acconci Stars and Strips." *Art in America* 64 (November–December 1976): 92–93.

Sondheim, Alan. "Vito Acconci Work 1973–1974." *Arts Magazine* 49 (March 1975): 49–52.

Staniszewski, Mary Anne. "New York Reviews: Acconci, Morris, Oppenheim." *Art News* 79 (September 1980): 348–49.

Stephano, Effie. "Image Changes: Effie Stephano Interviews Vito Acconci." *Art and Artists* 8 (February 1974): 24–27.

Stevens, Mark. "The Art of Shocking." *Newsweek* 95 (April 28, 1980): 95.

Vito Acconci, exhibition catalog. Lucern: Kunstmuseum, 1978.

Collision House, 1981
Installation at Max Protetch Gallery, New York
Bicycle, corrugated steel, pulley system
Dimensions variable

Like many other artists who came to prominence in the avant-garde of the mid-1960s, Vito Acconci worked out of Modernist formal traditions and under the pervasive influence of the Minimalist aesthetic. First as a poet, then as a figure on the visual art scene, Acconci followed the prevailing reductive aesthetic's inquiry into the material properties and abstract structure of things. For example, he used words in his poetry as if they were objects rather than signifiers, in order to "cover a space rather than uncover a meaning".[1] Eventually his exploration of words and language structure led to his involvement in the visual arts as he photographed basic activities, such as walking or stepping, in three-dimensional space. As a visual artist, Acconci differed from most contemporaneous sculptors primarily in his choice of material: while they concerned themselves with the manipulation of materials, aspects of process, and issues of objecthood, Acconci used his own body as his plastic medium, employing it to explore aspects of interpersonal relationships and issues of selfhood. His methodology was pure Minimal—very basic and clinical in its approach.

In the 1969 *Following Piece,* for instance, each day for several weeks Acconci randomly selected a person on the street whom he would then follow, undetected, everywhere throughout the day, observing whatever his subject did, until he lost the subject or was by circumstances prevented from further pursuit. Like any Minimalist art, *Following Piece* had a definite beginning and end which delimited it in time and space; although its duration was not predetermined, it could be described as systemically fixed. If the subject's activities were unpredictable, or "random" in their art context, the artist's were not, for they too were systemically fixed: he followed and observed, not unlike a clinician. Acconci's intention was not to intimidate or even to be "found out" by the subject; in fact, there was little eventfulness to *Following Piece,* whose structure, i.e., *form,* was utterly Minimal.

What is it, then, about *Following Piece* that makes it so terribly compelling, so nearly perverse, in its import? Surely it is not its structure: in going about their daily activities, individuals may inadvertently follow other individuals for some time, becoming aware of doing so belatedly or not at all, without evoking our distress or disapproval. Nor does the sinister aura of *Following Piece* stem from any malevolent intent on Acconci's part; his "interest" in his subject was patently mechanical and innocuous. Rather, what we find upsetting, and interesting, in *Following Piece* is its transgression of the culture-specific value of privacy; in our society the act of deliberately following another person *per se* is considered pernicious, regardless of its intention. *Following Piece,* like all of Acconci's work, derives its meaningfulness less from its form than from the cultural context in which it occurs. Thus, the physical forms that his works take, whether they are activities or installations like the recent constructions, deliver content which does not inhere in those forms but which is superinduced and must be communicated metaphorically. And although Acconci is somewhat reluctant to describe his works as metaphor, lest doing so should dismiss their "realness" as performed activities or actual objects to be reckoned with, he acknowledges that they do divulge their meaning metaphorically.

The conventional wisdom—and it is formidable—about Acconci's oeuvre is that it is fundamentally an examination of the political structure of interpersonal relationships at both an individual and a societal level. Acconci does not deal primarily with institutional or formalized relationships—such as marriage, business, or familial structures—but with the more elusive and invidious ones whereby people establish their behavior and, to a certain extent, their identities relative to one another—relationships such as leader/follower, giver/receiver, young/old, male/female, and so on. Acconci's early work was very much preoccupied with exploring the boundaries of the self—not of individual self, but of self*hood,* its sovereignty and its violability.

In *Following Piece* two independent agents went about their independent business; yet the artist's identity—his thoughts, his behavior, his activities—in effect was determined by the vagaries of the situation which he precipitated. Similarly, the moment-to-moment "identity" of the subject doubtless would have been altered had he known he was being followed and observed. In either case, the social, psychological, and physical behavior of each of the "independent" agents is affected by the knowledge of the other. Implicit in *Following Piece* is the notion that personal "identity" is not a core set of absolute and abiding "natural" traits and values, but rather a succession of moment-to-moment adaptations of behavior and attitudes to an ever-changing set of external circumstances. The outward manifestation of the "self," or personality, is a jumble of equivocal *personae,* all of which are valid expressions of the eternal fluidity of self.

In Acconci's scheme, selfhood is a kind of force field in which identities are exchangeable or transferable among others. Acconci's exploration of this faintly mystical idea gave rise to some of his most notorious early works, such as *Rubbings* (1970), *Project for Pier 17* (1971), and *Seedbed* (1972). These works, like many of his others, can be seen (and sometimes were) as harmless folly or outrageous affront. Acconci, like many of his perceptive critics, sees a humor in them (a humor not much written about), but conceives of them primarily as a very serious inquiry into the nature of selfhood. In *Rubbings* he placed a live cockroach onto his belly and rubbed it into his skin until there was no more cockroach, at least no physical evidence of it. The roach, of course, neither ceased to exist nor magically vanished, but continued to exist as an acknowledged presence through the person of the artist. Artist and roach both retained their *virtual* identity though they ostensibly had become one physical entity. Each can be said to have become metaphoric of the other, one reality carried by and revealed through the other.

In other works Acconci examined how he could dominate both the space of his activities and the spectators who witnessed it through the authority of his own personality. In *Project for Pier 17* Acconci stationed himself at an abandoned pier for a scheduled hour every night for a month; he would divulge to anybody who chose to meet him there a secret about his personal life or information which would embarrass or be detrimental to him if it were told to others. Acconci, playing either upon a voyeuristic impulse or the sincere good faith of his audience, co-opted them into his guilty secret and made them complicitous with it. To reveal or not to reveal what he had told them became a genuine moral question for those he involved, whether they bargained for it or not. And in *Seedbed,* surely his most controversial work, he lay masturbating under a ramp constructed in the gallery, inventing sexual fantasies (which he announced over a loudspeaker) about the sometimes unsuspecting gallery-goers who strode the boards above him.

In all these vintage works Acconci enacted an encroachment, a confrontation, or an exchange of identity with an unassuming other: the roach "became" the artist; the transgressions and guilt of the artist became those of his audience; the gallery visitor nonvolitionally became somebody else's wet dream. Manipulation, domination, and complicity, the substance of Acconci's politics, remain the overt focus of his current projects, but now played out at a societal and cultural level, rather than at an interpersonal one. Since the mid-1970s Acconci has been conspicuously absent from his works, preferring instead to take a more detached and satiric look at the politics of societal workings. No less theatrical than his conceptual performances, Acconci's mobile houses, vehicles, and what he calls the "self-erecting structures" that he has been making since 1979 are designed to allow the viewer/participant to take an active role in setting up physical metaphors for societal/political/sexual transactions. As for the artist, he emerges as a Picabian prankster, as in *Gang Bang* of 1980, an activity for ten automobiles: the roofs of nine of them were equipped with "inflatables" made of military camouflage fabric in the shape of penises which increased in size the faster the cars were driven; on the tenth car was another "inflatable" made from a parachute, in the shape of a breast. The vehicles were driven around the city of Spoleto (until they were banned), racing and chasing the object(s) of their desire. *Gang Bang,* as American in sensibility as it is comic, makes a public spectacle of our national game of equating things military, automotive, and sexual.

Acconci makes a similarly metaphoric use of the image of the house in two works of 1981, *Peeling House* and *Abstract House.* In these, a rudimentary house shape is outfitted with roller-shade-like walls bearing pop-art-like ideological insignias—stars and stripes, hammer and sickle, a Jewish star, a cross, and the like. The participation of the viewer

Fan City, 1981
Installation at Hirshhorn Museum and Sculpture Garden
Metal-and-cloth construction with pulleys, sash cord, and wood grips
Overall dimensions of site approx. 8.5 × 10.7 (28 × 35)

(itself a metaphor for complicity) is enlisted to operate these decorated shades, raising or lowering them to reveal their "true" identities. But these are ideological jack-in-the-boxes which surprise the viewer: in *Peeling House,* layer after layer of this happy-hued and merrily decorated shelter is peeled away to reveal a large stylized swastika lurking at its heart.

As is explicit in *Peeling House,* Acconci perceives decoration and other outward symbols of personal "identity" as propaganda. "The way one decorates a house," he reflects, "now becomes a sign for the decorator's relation to a culture. In that sense decoration is incredibly perverse. . . . it's the person being incredibly manipulated by the particular culture. . . . Decoration is a real political act."[2] This theme is continued in *Fan City,* Acconci's project for the present exhibition. It consists of an arrangement of four units that can be opened like fans to form a circle—a city—of tents, each "decorated" or identified by ideological and sociological banners.

Detail of *Fan City*

Like Acconci's other recent works, this project involves the active participation of the audience, requiring in this case the teamwork of two or more consenting viewers. Working together, as many as sixteen people bring *Fan City* from its "dormant" or closed state to a full disclosure of its hidden content. In its unopened state, *Fan City* consists of what appear to be four upright aluminum wedges anchored to a central mast at right angles to one another. Their shape is richly suggestive, described by the artist variously as the tail of a B-52 bomber, a shark's fin, or a beached whale—symbols of aggression or power immobilized. The stationary arrangement is activated in two stages. In the first, each of the units may be pulled open like a fan by one person's carrying it a quarter-circle around and thereby setting up the aluminum frames of three abutting pup-tent-like structures. As each "fan" is opened, a counterweight system erects half of a life-sized human silhouette—a kind of "Everyman" figure—along the mast. In the second stage of activation, anyone standing at the opening of a tent frame may pull on a black cord threaded through a pulley system which unfurls and pulls into position a pair of brightly colored nylon pennants to form the sides of the tent. Each pair of pennants (fashioned in the style of the all-American cheerleader pennant) bears not the name of an all-American team but a neutral-to-unflattering designation for social groups of various kinds: "Beggars," "Cripples," "Old Folks," "Blacks," "Aliens," "Pinkos," "Gays," "Punks," "Nymphos," "Schizos," "Junkies," "Freaks." All-American, indeed, Acconci's mildly offensive joke is short-lived; as the pull-cords are released, the pennants automatically retract on their spring rollers, and the wedges, when released, roll back to their closed position, lowering the "Everyman" figures. *Fan City* is now set to surprise its next group of visitors.

Acconci's own loyalties in this bit of name-calling remain ambiguous, but his witty intention is clear. While *Fan City's* inhabitants are identified by the familiar cheerleader pennants, those inhabitants are social groups, or "types," that American society at large would seem to prefer to forget about; in *Fan City* everybody is an outcast. In its examination of the relationship of a culture to those whose identity is manipulated by that culture, *Fan City* advances the frontier of Acconci's consideration of interpersonal politics to the realm of societal fascism.

Such are the overt concerns of Acconci's metaphorical art. Most, if not all, of what has been written in the impressive body of critical literature that has grown up about Acconci's work since the politically active 1960s has treated its political, social, and sexual content—an appropriate focus, since Acconci clearly has addressed these issues in his work. Underlying his political vision, however, a somewhat covert or sublimated religious strain appears to run through this body of often autobiographical work. It is worth noting that Acconci's speculations on the sovereignty and exchangeability of the self closely parallel such traditional Catholic concerns as free will, the soul, transubstantiation, and culpability. It is a Catholic sensibility that pervades his work.

Acconci, who attended Catholic schools until he was 22 and regularly attended Mass and took Communion, has reflected on the possible religious content of his work: "I sometimes wonder whether the isolation-chamber effect of my early artwork had anything to do with the confessional box. And, yes, it's just possible that the sexual currents you see in my work may have something to do with a Catholic upbringing. But these things are so hard to gauge."[3] Indeed so, yet there is rich evidence that Acconci's vision relates to issues beyond the transactional mechanics of social relationships.

Certainly the *Project for Pier 17* was patterned after Confession, but in this case there neither was nor could have been absolution; Acconci's guilt remained with him even though he had shared or "infected" another person with his culpability in a secular reenactment of original sin—the sharing of the *knowledge* of sin. And *Rubbings* may count as a somewhat questionable acting out of transubstantiation, in which the body and blood of one being become that of another. Even *Fan City* seems to have a one-to-one—albeit inverted—relationship with the Church. *Fan City* is everything that Vatican City is not: *Fan City* is built of prosaically modern materials—nylon and aluminum—and modeled in the form of the most nomadic of dwellings, the tent; it is shifting and indefinite in form, completely contingent for its moment-to-moment existence on the whim and willfulness of the casual viewer who sporadically fills the void caused by the absence of any abiding authority; the system of values it symbolically displays is hardly immutable—it can be altered by caprice or even by accident. This observation by no means suggests

Fan City

that Acconci is in any way blaspheming the Church or its theology; to the contrary, Acconci seems to have learned his catechism well, invoking its concerns, perhaps subconsciously, like a litany throughout his work.

Reviewing his development from the early works in which he isolated himself through the recent vehicles and houses, Acconci has suggested that the early pieces "were much more single-key whereas the later pieces seem to want to bring in different things, such as sex and politics. They are much more multiple-key pieces. If you are going to contrast comedy and tragedy, tragedy is single-keyed. Comedy allows you to have a serious and a laughing attitude at the same time. Comedy is about crowds; tragedy is about one person alone with his God who doesn't answer."[4] It appears that Acconci's recent work represents an adaptation to the circumstance of his unresponsive God. The political vision of a work such as *Fan City* is predicated on a Faustian vision of the self as completely plastic and capable of assuming endless incarnations. For Acconci, the creation of the self seems to be a determined and perservering act of will. Like modern philosophers from Nietzsche to Sartre, he asserts the creation of the self as the supreme artistry. Working through and within a discernible religious context, Acconci continues his evolution of a very personal, quintessentially secular, and not entirely un-divine comedy.

Notes

1. Vito Acconci, "Vito Acconci," *Avalanche,* no. 6 (Fall 1972; special Acconci issue):4.

2. Jan Avgikos, "Interview: Vito Acconci," *Art Papers* 5 (January/February 1981): 2–3.

3. Ellen Schwartz, "Vito Acconci: 'I Want to Put the Viewer on Shaky Ground'," *Art News* 80 (Summer 1981): 98.

4. Avgikos, "Interview," p. 3.

Fan City

Siah Armajani

Born in Teheran, Iran, July 10, 1939.
Moved to U.S., 1960.
Became U.S. citizen, 1967.
Lives in Minneapolis.

Reading House, 1980
Wood, shingles, plexiglass, paint
4.9 × 9.8 × 6.7 (16 × 32 × 22)

Education

B.A., Macalester College, St. Paul, Minnesota, 1963.

Awards

National Endowment for the Arts Artists Fellowship, 1978.

Selected Solo Exhibitions

Moore College of Art, Philadelphia, 1977.

Courthouse Square, Cooperative Workshop, Wright State University, Dayton, Ohio, 1977.

Philadelphia College of Art, 1978.

Max Protetch Gallery, New York, 1978, 1981.

Ohio State University, Columbus, 1979.

Contemporary Arts Center, Cincinnati, 1980.

Joslyn Art Museum, Omaha, 1980.

The Hudson River Museum, Yonkers, New York, 1981.

Baxter Art Gallery, California Institute of Technology, Los Angeles, 1982.

Selected Group Exhibitions

Art by Telephone, Museum of Contemporary Art, Chicago, 1969.

Towers, Museum of Contemporary Art, Chicago, 1969, and tour, 1969–70.

Painting and Sculpture Today—1969, Indianapolis Museum of Art, 1969.

Art in the Mind, Allen Art Museum, Oberlin College, Oberlin, Ohio, 1970.

Information, The Museum of Modern Art, New York, 1970.

Works for New Spaces, Walker Art Center, Minneapolis, 1971.

Documenta V, Kassel, West Germany, 1972.

Discussions: Works/Words, The Clocktower, Institute for Art and Urban Resources, New York, 1974.

16 Projects/4 Artists: Siah Armajani, Larry Bell, Lloyd Hamrol, Pat Steir, Wright State University, Dayton, Ohio, 1976, and tour, 1976–77.

Virtual Reality, Carpenter Center for the Visual Arts, Harvard University, Cambridge, Massachusetts, 1976.

Scale and Environment: 10 Sculptors, Walker Art Center, Minneapolis, 1977.

Young American Artists: 1978 Exxon National Exhibition, Solomon R. Guggenheim Museum, New York, 1978.

Architectural Analogues, Whitney Museum of American Art, Downtown Branch, New York, 1978.

Dwellings, Institute of Contemporary Art, University of Pennsylvania, Philadelphia, 1978.

Art and Architecture: Space and Structure, Protetch-McIntosh Gallery, Washington, D.C., 1979.

Wave Hill: The Artist's View, Wave Hill, Bronx, New York, 1979.

Fifth Bridge, 1979
Installation at Neuberger Museum, Purchase, New York
Wood, corrugated steel, stain
3.6 × 27.4 × 11 (12 × 90 × 36)

Will Brown

Model for *Louis Kahn Lecture Room,* 1981
Proposal for permanent installation at Fleisher Art Memorial, Philadelphia submitted for Fairmount Park Art Association's Tricentennial program *Form and Function: Projects for Philadelphia*
Balsam

Text from Walt Whitman's "Song of Myself":

When the materials are all prepared and ready the architects shall appear.
The greatest among them shall be he who best knows you,
and encloses all and is faithful to all,
he and the rest shall not forget you,
they shall perceive that you are not an iota less than they,
you shall be fully glorified in them.

Venice Biennale, 1980.

Environmental Art, XIII Winter Olympic Games, Lake Placid, New York, 1980.

Architectural Sculpture, Los Angeles Institute of Contemporary Art, 1980.

Biennial Exhibition, Whitney Museum of American Art, New York, 1981.

Selected Bibliography

Ashbery, John. "Trashing the Sixties." *New York* 11 (May 29, 1978): 64–65.

Berlind, Robert. "Armajani's Open-Ended Structures." *Art in America* 67 (October 1979): 82–85.

Brown, Julie. *Siah Armajani,* exhibition catalog. Yonkers, N.Y.: Hudson River Museum, 1981.

Chapin, Louis. " 'Against Art': 'Information' Display." *Christian Science Monitor,* July 22, 1970, p. 8.

Day, Holliday T. *I-80 Series: Siah Armajani: Reading Garden #2,* exhibition catalog. Omaha: Joslyn Art Museum, 1980.

Finch, Christopher. "Process and Imagination." *Design Quarterly,* nos. 74–75 (1969).

Jordan, James. "Artist/Artificer/Armajani." *Dialogue,* January–February 1981, pp. 7–8.

Kardon, Janet, and Armajani, Siah. *Projects for PCA: Siah Armajani: Red School House for Thomas Paine,* exhibition catalog. Philadelphia: Philadelphia College of Art, 1978.

Klein, Michael R. "Siah Armajani." In *Scale and Environment: 10 Sculptors,* exhibition catalog, pp. 16–21. Minneapolis: Walker Art Center, 1977.

Koshalek, Richard. "A New Idiom of Public Art." *Landscape Architecture* 61 (July 1971): 313–16.

Larson, Kay. "Art: Spring Cleaning: Siah Armajani." *New York* 14 (March 30, 1981):49.

Levin, Kim. "House and Gardens." *Village Voice,* July 1–7, 1981, pp. 77–78.

Lippard, Lucy R. *Dwellings,* exhibition catalog. Philadelphia: Institute of Contemporary Art, University of Pennsylvania, 1978.

———. *Six Years: The Dematerialization of the Art Object from 1966 to 1972,* pp. 163, 204. New York: Praeger Publishers, 1973.

McShine, Kynaston L., ed. *Information,* exhibition catalog. New York: The Museum of Modern Art, 1970.

Pincus-Witten, Robert. "Siah Armajani: Populist Mechanics." *Arts Magazine* 53 (October 1978): 126–28.

Shapiro, David. "Mr. Processionary at the Conceptacle." *Art News* 69 (September 1970): 58–61.

Shearer, Linda. *Young American Artists: 1978 Exxon National Exhibition,* exhibition catalog, pp. 14–18. New York: Solomon R. Guggenheim Museum, 1978.

Spurlock, William, ed. *16 Projects/4 Artists: Siah Armajani, Larry Bell, Lloyd Hamrol, Pat Steir,* exhibition catalog. Dayton, Ohio: Wright State University, 1979.

Stone, Michele, and Sky, Alison. *Unbuilt America.* New York: McGraw-Hill Publishers, 1976.

Thomson, Pat. "Constructions I: Siah Armajani." *Dialogue,* November–December 1980, pp. 56–57.

"To build open, available, useful, low, near, common, public gathering places. Gathering places which are neighborly."[1] This clear-minded and succinct statement by Siah Armajani is a near-distillation of his current aspirations as an artist and a humanist. It specifies both the physical form—open, low, public—and the ideal value—available, useful, common—of the structures he has been building for the past five years. Armajani variously describes his work as architectural sculpture, pure architecture, environmental sculpture; the taxonomy, however, does not really matter: "It is art/architecture," says Armajani. "I have lost sight of the differences; I no longer know what separates them." Indeed, in his case it is hard to know, but his recent constructions, which are built from an architectural concept and to an architectural scale, have become increasingly more inviting of human activity—more *functional*—and it is certainly possible to think of them as architecture. For Armajani, architecture, and especially public architecture, is the most humanistic of art forms, capable both of revealing the values and ideals of a particular culture and of enacting or realizing those values through its applied use as a tool of that culture. Thus his architecture is at once theory and praxis, idea and reality, concept and object. His reading gardens, lecture rooms, and gathering places at once articulate an American democratic idealism that has long been central to his artistic vision and serve to put those values to work.

Although Armajani acknowledges that the nature of an individual's experience of space may indeed be a valid aesthetic experience (as it was and is for many sculptors), the simple phenomenology of space is not enough to motivate his work, which instead comes from his sense of a loftier purpose for art than the idle delectation of artificial space. "My intent is to build something which is a 'necessity of thought,' " explains Armajani, quoting Martin Heidegger, "and not merely problematic and accidental: something which relates to human purposes, something which applies to being with things and, along with others, belonging to a place." *Necessity of thought* indeed seems to be the ideological rationale for Armajani's numerous projects and for his development in general since the mid-1960s. After graduation from Macalester College in St. Paul, Minnesota, where he had come from his native Iran, Armajani continued to study philosophy while he pursued a career as a painter. Like many young artists during those years, however, he found the dominant formalist aesthetics incompatible with his wish to address his work to his deepest concerns. As he explained in an interview with Linda Shearer: "In 1966 I was studying philosophy and realized that there were so many ideas which I could not express in my painting. I was terribly dissatisfied with these paintings. . . . This dissatisfaction was based on the conclusion that there were certain ideas, not only philosophical ones, which could not be translated or expressed directly in the forms of painting and sculpture as they existed then. What was needed was a reinvestigation of art."[2]

It may be a reflection on the depleted vitality of that prevalent aesthetic that Armajani, like many of his contemporaries, found it so constraining that his reinvestigation turned him away from anything like classically defined painting or sculpture. It brought him to architecture. Armajani's first nonpainted works were conceptual pieces for various towers, such as a proposal for a tower that would be tall enough to cast its shadow across the entire state of North Dakota; although the piece is plainly fantastical, it is significant that the shadow, an immaterial phenomenon, was as critical to the piece as the tower, whose only reason for existence was to produce the shadow; it is almost as if the shadow created the huge tower. A similarly conceptual motivation seems to have been responsible for a series of curious miniature and full-scale bridges that Armajani built from the late 1960s to the mid-'70s. Large or small, all these bridges were equally impractical, and Armajani considered them in either scale to be "whole" works of art—a miniature bridge was not less a bridge than one that could be traversed by a person—because they were actual, physically realized entities constructed between two points on a continuous line which were thereby "connected." One of the full-scale projects, *Bridge Over a Nice Triangle Tree* (1970), connected no two *particular* points but simply conducted the traveller to a stairway leading up one side of the tree and down the other. Undeniably, the structure was a bridge, connecting two points and spanning a body, and it demonstrated the defining qualities of a bridge. In fact all of Armajani's bridges, regardless of their size, were *models,* not in the sense of their being preliminary small-scale replicas or maquettes for proposed "real" bridges, but rather as theoretical projections of possible systems

Hirshhorn Employee Lounge, 1981
Installation at Hirshhorn Museum and Sculpture Garden
Painted wood construction
Overall dimensions of site approx. 8.5 × 10.7 (28 × 35)

Text excerpted from Walt Whitman's poetry

The axe leaps!
The solid forest
Gives fluid utterances,
They tumble forth,
They rise and form,
Hut, tent, landing, survey,
Flail, plough, pick,
Crowbar, spade,
Shingle, rail, prop, wainscot,
Jamb, lath, panel, gable,
Citadel, ceiling, saloon, academy,
Organ, exhibition-house, library,
Cornice, trellis, pilaster,
Balcony, window,
Turrent, porch,
Hoe, rake, pitchfork, pencil,
Wagon, staff, saw,
Jack-plane, mallet,
Wedge, rounce,
Chair, tub, hoop, table,
Wicket, vane, sash, floor,
Work-box, chest,
String'd instrument,
Boat, frame, and what not.

Unscrew the lock from the doors!
Unscrew the doors themselves from their jambs!

The big doors of the country-barn
Stand open and ready,
The dried grass of the harvest-time
Loads the slow-drawn wagon.
The clear light plays on the brown gray
And green intertinged,
The armfuls are packed
To the sagging mow.
Within their walls
Shall all that forwards perfect human
Life be started,
Tried, taught, advanced. Visibly exhibited.

This is the grass that grows
Wherever the land is
and the water is
This is the common air
that bathes the globe
It is for the endless races
of working people
and farmers and seamen.

of bridge-building "syntax." All of Armajani's bridges emphasized, like a skeleton, each of the structural elements that together conspired to synthesize the total or whole structure of the bridge. They were like Platonic ideal bridges, defining models for the structure and system of all bridges and depictions of no particular bridge whatsoever. They stand for the *language* of the bridge and its *concept.* Similar concerns led Armajani to produce a series of exaggerated models of such basic architectural elements as the door, the gable, the wall, and the window, bearing the collective title *Dictionary of Building* (1973–78). Like the bridges, the works are analogous to anatomical models of bodies and body parts used for medical instruc-

Detail of *Hirshhorn Employee Lounge*

Detail of *Hirshhorn Employee Lounge*

tion. They serve as prototypes or schematics of anatomical and structural principles. A bridge or window that serves no practical purpose can only be thought about, as if it were a concept; it is evident that this is precisely what Armajani intended.

The *Dictionary,* a somewhat underestimated project in Armajani's oeuvre, provided the physical and conceptual foundations for his next group of significant works, a series of "houses" synthesized from syntactical principles found in the vocabulary of the *Dictionary.* The purpose of these uninhabitable houses was conceptual and analytical of the properties and conditions of "houseness." *Thomas Jefferson's House, West Wing, Sunset House,* for example, was plainly not intended as a depiction of or a maquette for any real house, but was loosely based on the underlying principles of Jefferson's plans for Monticello. This disjunctive sequence of architectural fragments—windows, rooms, walls, a corridor, and other elements of a house—has the overall effect of a collection of parts rather than an organically arranged and homogeneous entity. This house must be explored from all vantage points and assimilated piecemeal; it cannot be "known" except by direct, firsthand exploration and deliberate rumination. Robert Berlind has astutely summarized Armajani's aesthetic strategy: "His mode is inductive and anti-hieratic. Each disjunctive movement is, in a way, like a Brechtian aside, where the action is interrupted and reflection is urged. Where the Baroque mode is authoritarian and often seductive, Armajani's presents itself as populist and tolerant of disengagement. . . . To provide a clear gestalt would preclude the kind of dialogue he hopes to initiate with his public."[3] Thus, Armajani's architecture functions as a kind of real-time drama that plays out the aesthetic tension between object and idea, between diverse parts and overall scheme, between being and becoming.

During Armajani's early investigation of architecture, he developed a specific interest in early American "vernacular" architecture and in building types such as log cabins, covered bridges, and Shaker meetinghouses. He admired these structures for their simplicity of form, their use of common and homely materials, and their application of straightforward building techniques that stressed efficiency, strength, and economy of means. To Armajani this architecture represented a direct expression of certain American ideals and values: a kind of self-evident truthfulness to materials and building techniques; self-sufficiency; accessibility—physical, visual, and intellectual; practicality; and an authentically American style and character. In such bridges, houses, and meeting rooms each element of the construction was essential and could not be compromised; form was determined solely by function and there was no hierarchical subordination of doors, windows and roofs to dramatic porticoes, stately capitals, or other accouterments of grandeur. The physical forms of such mountain and prairie architecture impressed Armajani as direct expressions of—or at least physical analogues or metaphors for—American culture and democratic ideals, and Armajani recognized them as appropriate expressive and imaginative models for many of his philosophical concerns. "This democratic approach deeply appeals to me," he later commented. "You know, I really see myself as a midwestern populist."[4]

Armajani's affinity for the populist ideal and the simple utilitarian architecture he sees as its embodiment remained with him throughout the period of his architecture-related conceptual works, and has forcefully asserted itself in the functionality of his recent reading rooms and gathering places.

Just as his architecture has developed from concept to object and from single elements to complexly related groups of elements, so does this additive thrust now allow for the incorporation of functional aspects of the architectural models it presents. There is nothing in the functionality of a reading room or a gathering place that controverts its conceptual basis; to the contrary, *use* in Armajani's democratic idiom completes the concept of his architectural investigations. American pragmatism is as appropriate to the *result* of an Armajani structure as it is to its *concept.*

In speaking about his work, Armajani sometimes makes an analogy between empty or unused architecture and an empty jug: when filled, the jug is not less of a jug; in fact, using it gives the jug its *significance.*

Detail of *Hirshhorn Employee Lounge*

So it has become with Armajani's architecture. Its usage establishes a kind of covenant or community between artist and audience, and forges a continuity of art experience and ordinary experience in a manner that does not occur as an accidental convenience for the audience/users but which is the artist's assertion of the potential significance of all experience. For Armajani, use represents the actual fulfillment of his democratic principles.

A structure such as *Hirshhorn Employee Lounge,* Armajani's project for this exhibition, is conceived as a functioning lounge for the Hirshhorn Museum's employees and their guests, the general public. This environment is not a single open space but is divided by the benches and tables that are characteristic of Armajani's style into several "islands" that afford semi-enclosed spaces for solitude and privacy or areas for small gatherings. There are places to hang one's hat, bookshelves, and a

Hirshhorn Employee Lounge

stylized mantelpiece—all cultural icons connoting rest and comfort. Significantly there is no distinct barrier between the somewhat public or communal environment and the private zones; rather, they flow one into the other. The *Lounge* is a place for rest, contemplation, and relaxed conversation, an environment for practical, if leisurely, activities.

Armajani is quick to point out his agreement with Martin Heidegger that practical activities are not "atheoretical" but have "their own sort of vision"—a "vision" expressed here as a built environment that represents "a synthesis of ideological and structural concerns." Armajani would describe the *Lounge* as "a commonsense building," meaning that it "is not the sum of the materials which go to make it up," but "is presupposed by every object within it. Its immediate concern is not with the physical object of the building, but with the work which it is meant to perform. The commonsense building is a referential structure to serve the people. It adapts itself to human hands."

For Armajani, the noblest and most practical effort of human hands, the most exalted and commonsensical work, is *building*—building not just *things* but cities, nations, civilizations. The evolution of Armajani's own work thus far has been from concept to model to usable building, from the rudiments of building to the full flourishing of the significance of building. The idealistic spirit with which Armajani has fulfilled this undertaking is perhaps best related verbally in the exultant passage from Walt Whitman's "Song of the Broad-Axe" inscribed on the walls of the *Lounge*. It is a rhapsody to building—to tools, to work, to the things that are built. The excerpted passage begins with the axe and the tree and progresses to an incantation of the things that are built, from the crude and stationary hut to the surging steamboat and sailing clipper. With Whitman, Armajani rejoices in the commonsense miracle of the builder: in his hands "The axe leaps! . . . The shapes arise!"

Hirshhorn Employee Lounge

Notes

1. This and subsequent uncited statements by Armajani are from an unpublished interview conducted by Melanie Taylor and Toby Engelberg in 1981.

2. Linda Shearer, untitled interview with the artist in *Young American Artists: 1978 Exxon National Exhibition,* exhibition catalog (New York: Solomon R. Guggenheim Museum, 1978), p. 14.

3. Robert Berlind, "Armajani's Open-Ended Structures," *Art in America* 67 (October 1979): 84.

4. Shearer, p. 14.

Alice Aycock

Born in Harrisburg, Pennsylvania, November 20, 1946.
Lives in New York.

Education

B.A., Douglass College, Rutgers University, New Brunswick, New Jersey, 1968.
M.A., Hunter College, New York, 1971.

Awards

National Endowment for the Arts Artists Fellowship, 1976, 1980.
Creative Artists Public Service Grant, 1976.

Selected Solo Exhibitions

Nova Scotia College of Art and Design, Halifax, 1972.

112 Greene Street, New York, 1974, 1977.

Artpark, Lewiston, New York, 1977.

The Museum of Modern Art, New York, 1977.

Portland (Oregon) Center for the Visual Arts, 1978.

Galleria Salvatore Ala, Milan, 1978.

Cranbrook Academy of Art, Bloomfield Hills, Michigan, 1978.

Philadelphia College of Art, 1978.

Muhlenberg College, Allentown, Pennsylvania, 1978.

John Weber Gallery, 1978, 1979, 1981.

Contemporary Arts Center, Cincinnati, 1979.

Protetch-McIntosh Gallery, Washington, D.C., 1979.

P.S.1, Institute for Art and Urban Resources, New York, 1980.

Washington Project for the Arts, Washington, D.C., 1980.

University of South Florida, Tampa, 1981.

Selected Group Exhibitions

9e Biennale de Paris, Musée d'art moderne de la ville de Paris, 1975.

Documenta VI, Kassel, West Germany, 1977.

Metaphor and Illusion, Wright State University, Dayton, Ohio, 1977.

Architectural Analogues, Whitney Museum of American Art, Downtown Branch, New York, 1978.

Dwellings, Institute of Contemporary Art, University of Pennsylvania, Philadelphia, 1978.

Made by Sculptors, Stedelijk Museum, Amsterdam, 1978.

Venice Biennale, 1978, 1980.

Art and Architecture: Space and Structure, Protetch-McIntosh Gallery, Washington, D.C., 1979.

Biennial Exhibition, Whitney Museum of American Art, New York, 1979, 1981.

The Decade in Review, Whitney Museum of American Art, New York, 1979.

From the Series Entitled "The Miraculating Machine: Mock Suns and Halos 'Round the Moon," 1981
Installation at the Institute for Contemporary Art, University of Pennsylvania, Philadelphia, created for *Machineworks* exhibition
Aluminum, barbed wire, brass cymbals, copper, galvanized sheet steel, glass, grinding discs, latex, monofilament, motors, nichrome, plastic, porcelain, rubber, sandblasted black steel pipe, sandblasted mild steel, sandblasted steel plate, silicon carbide, solenoids, spring steel, steel cable, timers
9.1 × 7.6 × 15.2 (30 × 25 × 50)

International Sculpture Conference, Washington, D.C., 1980.

Aycock, Holste, Singer, The Fort Worth Art Museum, 1980.

Architectural Sculpture, Los Angeles Institute of Contemporary Art, 1980.

Art on the Beach, Battery Park Landfill, New York, 1980.

Collaboration: Artists and Architects, New York Historical Society, New York, 1981.

Machineworks: Vito Acconci, Alice Aycock, Dennis Oppenheim, Institute for Contemporary Art, University of Pennsylvania, Philadelphia, 1981.

Mythos und Ritual in der Kunst der 70er Jahre, Kunsthaus Zürich, 1981.

Selected Bibliography

Albright, Thomas. "Alice Aycock's Personal Flight of Fancy." *San Francisco Chronicle,* August 29, 1979, p. 54.
Aycock, Alice. "Notes on Project for a Simple Network for Underground Wells and Tunnels." In *Projects in Nature,* exhibition catalog. Far Hills, N.J.: Merriewold West, 1975.

Large Scale Dis/Integration of
Microelectronic Memories (A Newly Revised Shanty Town), 1980
Installation at Battery Park Landfill, New York (two views)
Wood and steel

Large Scale Dis/Integration of Microelectronic Memories (A Newly Revised Shanty Town) *is a series of complexes derived from several sequences of drawings. It is—like any city—a work in progress, a visionary megalopolis. In the initially constructed part of the project, which is based on the "Leaping Chasm" drawings from the "Paradise Romances" cycle, the viewer will be led across ramps, through mazes and into 22 partitioned compartments. The second part of the project shares its narrative predicate with the artist's "First City of the Dead: A City of Doors," from a story of an old woman who constructs a wall of 52 doors for each year of her life. Pacing the streets of the city she has built, the woman hopes to see her own history revealed to her. The plan for the new shanty city is based on a young woman's actual perambulations through the streets of New York. The new project is about enclosure and solitude and deprivation. It attempts to be impenetrable. It sets itself up as a lure. It becomes a trap . . . The New Shanty Town is a forbidden city. It is also an amusement park, a lunatic asylum, a prison house, a cemetery, a market-place, a battlefield, a labyrinth, a paradise.*
—Alice Aycock

The Savage Sparkler, 1981
Installation at State University College at Plattsburgh, Plattsburgh, New York
Fans, fluorescent lights, galvanized metal, rack of hot coils, steel
3 × 9.1 × 15.2 (10 × 30 × 50)

———. "Project for Five Wells Descending a Hillside." *Tracks* 2 (Spring 1976): 23–26.

———. "Work 1972–1974." In *Individuals: Post-Movement Art in America,* edited by Alan Sondheim, pp. 104–21. New York: E. P. Dutton & Co., 1977.

Bell, Jane. "New York Reviews: Alice Aycock (John Weber)." *Art News* 79 (February 1980): 199–200.

Boettger, Suzaan. "Environments for Experience." *Artweek* 10 (September 22, 1979): 1, 16.

Bourgeois, Jean-Louis. "Review of Exhibitions: New York: Alice Aycock at 112 Greene St." *Art in America* 65 (July–August 1977): 94.

Crary, Jonathan. "Projects in Nature." *Arts Magazine* 50 (December 1975): 52–53.

Denton, Monroe, introduction; Fry, Edward F., essay; and Morgan, Stuart, essay. *"after years of ruminating on the events that led him up to his misfortune . . . ": Alice Aycock: Projects and Proposals, 1971–1978,* exhibition catalog. Allentown, Pa.: Muhlenberg College, 1978.

Fleming, Lee. "Art Reviews: Alice Aycock: 'Game of Flyers,' WPA Art Site." *Washington Review* 5 (April–May 1980): 22.

Fry, Edward F., essay. *Alice Aycock: Projects 1979–1981,* exhibition catalog. Tampa: University of South Florida, 1981.

Kardon, Janet. "Janet Kardon Interviews Some Modern Maze-Makers: Interview with Alice Aycock, September 1975." *Art International* 20 (April–May 1976): 65–66.

———. *Projects for PCA: Alice Aycock: History of a Beautiful May Rose Garden in the Month of January,* exhibition catalog. Philadelphia: Philadelphia College of Art, 1978.

Keeffe, Jeffrey. "Reviews: New York: Alice Aycock, John Weber Gallery." *Artforum* 16 (May 1978): 64–65.

Kingsley, April. "Six Women at Work in the Landscape." *Arts Magazine* 52 (April 1978): 108–12.

Kuspit, Donald B. "Aycock's Dream Homes." *Art in America* 68 (September 1980): 84–87.

Larson, Kay. "Downtown, Alice Aycock." *Village Voice,* December 3, 1979, p. 96.

Lewis, Jo Ann. "Scanning the Sky." *Washington Post,* September 22, 1979, p. B7.

Lippard, Lucy R. *Dwellings,* exhibition catalog. Philadelphia: Institute of Contemporary Art, University of Pennsylvania, 1978.

———. *Six Years: The Dematerialization of the Art Object from 1966 to 1972.* New York: Praeger Publishers, 1973.

Lobell, John. "Myth in Architecture: The Work of Alice Aycock." *Skyline* 3 (April 1980): 6.

Lorber, Richard. "Reviews: New York: Alice Aycock, 112 Greene Street." *Artforum* 15 (Summer 1977): 64–65.

Machineworks: Vito Acconci, Alice Aycock, Dennis Oppenheim, exhibition catalog. Philadelphia: Institute of Contemporary Art, University of Pennsylvania, 1981.

Morgan, Stuart. "Reviews: New York: Alice Aycock, John Weber Gallery." *Artforum* 18 (January 1980): 64–65.

———. "Reviews: Philadelphia: 'Machineworks,' Institute of Contemporary Art." *Artforum* 19 (Summer 1981): 97–98.

———, and Aycock, Alice. "Alice Aycock: 'A Certain Image of Something I Like Very Much.' " *Arts Magazine* 52 (March 1978): 118–19.

Morris, Robert. "The Present Tense of Space." *Art in America* 66 (January–February 1978): 70.

Mythos und Ritual in der Kunst der 70er Jahre, exhibition catalog. Zurich: Kunsthaus Zürich, 1981.

Onorato, Ronald J. "The Modern Maze." *Art International* 20 (April–May 1976): 21–24.

Richard, Paul. "Stage Props in Search of a Pastime." *Washington Post,* February 23, 1980, pp. B1–2.

Rubinfien, Leo. "Reviews: New York: Alice Aycock, Museum of Modern Art." *Artforum* 16 (March 1978): 69–70.

Ryan, David. *Aycock, Holste, Singer,* exhibition catalog. Fort Worth: Fort Worth Art Museum, 1980.

Shapiro, David. "A View of Kassel." *Artforum* 16 (September 1977): 60, 62.

Sheffield, Margaret. "Alice Aycock: Mystery Under Construction." *Artforum* 16 (September 1977): 63–65.

Smith, Roberta. "Reviews: Alice Aycock, 112 Greene Street." *Artforum* 13 (September 1974): 71.

Wooster, Ann-Sargent. "Reviews: New York: Alice Aycock, 112 Greene Street." *Artforum* 14 (February 1976): 62, 63.

Wortz, Melinda. "University of California, Irvine." In *Architectural Sculpture: Projects,* exhibition catalog, pp. 38–42, 47–49. Los Angeles: Los Angeles Institute of Contemporary Art, 1980.

Hoodo (Laura). From the Series Entitled "How to Catch and Manufacture Ghosts." Vertical and Horizontal Cross-section of the Ether Wind., 1981
Installation at Hirshhorn Museum and Sculpture Garden
Copper, formica, galvanized sheet metal, glass, heating coils, incandescent light bulbs, iron, lead, motors, neon, steel, steel cable
Overall dimensions of site approx. 8.5 × 10.7 (28 × 35)

There is no machine powerful or grand or intricate enough to contain the terrible energy that Alice Aycock intends for her machines, which are fueled by nothing less than the infinite energy and intelligence that animates all creation. Indeed, Aycock's aspiration as an artist is to create a machine so charged with power that its ultimate destiny—and its sole purpose *as a work of art*—would be to spontaneously combust, to consume itself in an instant of energy, and vanish forever. And such a machine would have validity only as a work of art, or an act of faith, serving no purpose but to reveal that power. Until she can devise a machine capable of containing and disclosing the infinite (a goal that is unlikely to be reached), Alice Aycock must be content to approximate or simulate that energy through the kinds of fantastical constructions she has been making from a seemingly endless array of industrial apparatus for the past several years.

A random survey of her recent projects discovers such improbable machines as *The Miraculating Machine: Mock Suns and Halos 'Round the Moon*; *The Great God Pan*; *The Savage Sparkler*; *Rotary Lightning Express (An Apparatus for Determining the Effects of Mesmerism on the Terrestrial Currents)*; and *The Machine That Makes the World.* All of them, large or not-so-large, are remarkably complex agglomerations of discrete parts—motors, grinding discs, pulleys, glass tubes, metal drums, electrical conductors, fans, lights, etc.—which have been removed from their original functions and reconstituted into outlandish (and only potentially comprehensible) relationships.

Although we have been taught that machines are instruments of linear thought, engines of logic guided by purposeful mechanical principles, there is no rational purpose to be divined from all the goings-on in Aycock's machines; they are preposterous and mysterious contrivances that seem propelled not by measured and rational formulae but by madness—madness understood in its classical or prophetic sense as a state of inspiration. They are pure manifestations, actual flickerings, of that vital energy

Detail of *Hoodo (Laura)*

in which they share. Aycock intends for her machines to be seen not as depictions of or references to that energy, but rather as a living *part of* the continuum of that force. Thus Aycock's machines are not enclosed or segregated from the world but seem to permeate the whole of a space, animating it and radiating energy. The same force that drives the machine drives its creation and conception in the artist; the artist serves almost as a medium through which the awesome animating energy, flowing as creative energy, produces a machine which renders that energy physically, visually, and psychologically perceptible. For Aycock, who sees her work as something akin to alchemy or magic, there is an eternal mystery to the numberless protean states which this energy assumes.

Madness, mystery, and irrationality have long been critical aspects of Aycock's sculpture. Just as her recent machines use the rational vocabulary of machinery manifested irrationally, so many of her early architectural projects employed the rational methods of post-and-lintel construction to create notably disjunctive, incoherent, and ambiguous structures. Aycock's earliest works took such forms as mazes, catacomblike systems of underground wells and tunnels, tubular "buildings" with narrow ledges, and such bits of false architecture as a set of stairs that came to a dead end at the ceiling. Such obstacle courses and claustrophobic spaces, meant to be experienced by crawling or groping one's way through them, were essentially phenomenological in presentation. Original as they were, they reflected Aycock's tutelage by Robert Morris and her study of Gaston Bachelard's *The Poetics of Space;* both Morris and Bachelard stressed the bodily and sensate experience of space as a confrontation with one's whole physical and mental being.

But Aycock demanded a greater imaginative exercise in her art than her early spatial manipulations could provide, and her work quickly evolved to more complex macro-architecture. Around 1977 Aycock began a series of projects and proposals modeled after fortresses, walled towns, and cities. Although clearly imbued with the somewhat abstract aesthetics of spatial and

Detail of *Hoodo (Laura)*

architectural elements that had informed her previous works, these projects were distinctly more fantastical in their content and generally were accompanied by long, disjunctive texts that included quasinarrative scenarios, historical annotations, and remarks to the reader. For example, her 1978 *Project Entitled "On the Eve of the Industrial Revolution—A City Engaged in the Production of False Miracles"* featured five structures and a lengthy "program" which included twelfth- and fourteenth-century historical anecdotes and this curious instruction to the viewer: "Imagine the site as a place where children burn mysterious things." The text portion of another work called for mythological personages, deities, and even celestial bodies as the cast of characters for a play set simultaneously in twenty-eight cities from Toronto to Baghdad.

As it became clear to Aycock that even these literature-embellished architectural sculptures were strained by the imaginative overload with which she was investing them, the more cerebral and less archetypal icon of the machine asserted itself as the proper philosophical and metaphorical key to her work.

Donald B. Kuspit has observed that Aycock's architectural work developed from such "cellar" pieces as her early underground chambers to the "garret" pieces of a few years later, with their ladders, towers, and allusions to levitation. "Built by application of the 'Gothic' principle of juxtaposition," he reflects, "her pieces can be said to move from crypt to spire, suggesting at once inner sanctum and towering aspiration—an impacted dream of spiritual flight, inner escape to the beyond. They are a new reification of the sublime."[1] It may now be added that with the advent of her machines, Aycock's work has altogether moved out of the house, with its patently human history, launched by the machine into a more confounding realm—a realm of universal forces and suprarational order. The machine as Aycock has developed it—that is, as growing out of and subsuming the imaginative quotient of her architecture—suggests a *fugal* or *encyclopedic* development: her work in general has developed less as a sequence of phases than by the fluid accretion and assimilation of a canon of imaginative content that is absorbed, rather than replaced, by its continuing growth.

Aycock's transition to machine morphology seems to have been inevitable, for the images and inventions of the Industrial Revolution had already begun to appear—in the form of waterwheels, mills, and other primitive mechanical devices—in her outgrown architectural structures, supplanting the architectural framework that housed them. Most pieces of architecture—that is, most buildings—function as more or less passive containers in which some activity occurs. Some edifices, however, are themselves instruments and devices of that activity and essentially function as architecture-sized tools; structures from the pyramids and Stonehenge to cyclotrons and planetary observatories are in essence architectural machinery. They are purpose-built catalysts to and necessary components of some operation in or on the material world—an operation, such as the tracking of stars, that is made possible by their form. Their function is to translate or metamorphose something into something else. The morphology and purpose of the machine as an active transformer seems indeed to make it the "natural" icon and archetype of Aycock's art. Significantly, Aycock relates all of her machines to a tradition of cosmology and cosmographic representations of the physical and conceptual structure of the universe. Her machines are simultaneously manifestations of and metaphors for cosmic forces. Aycock's project for this exhibition, bearing the unwieldy title *Hoodo (Laura). From the Series Entitled "How to Catch and Manufacture Ghosts." Vertical and Horizontal Cross-section of the Ether Wind,* is in fact a kind of fantasia based upon several cosmological drawings. One of the drawings echoed here is an allegorical diagram by the seventeenth-century English mystical philosopher Robert Fludd depicting the universe as a monochord, or medieval instrument used for measuring and demonstrating mathematical relations of musical tones. Another is a Tantric diagram depicting the regions of the head, represented as a series of ovals and half-ellipses, penetrating into the cosmos. Other drawings were digested into the scheme of *Hoodo,* but these two, with their intersecting eccentric circles and ellipses, provided the visual and conceptual basis for the rings, broad discs, circular movements, and spirals everywhere at work in this fantastical machine.

The grand and mysterious contrivance consists of several elements which are neither clearly differentiated nor quite integrated into a single system, but are poised disjunctively and illogically. The central element is a large, hypnotically whirling spherical shape which closely resembles the kind of wind-driven rotary ventilator often seen on the roofs of buildings. This "mother image," as Aycock describes it, creates an updraft that she likens to "ether wind," an all-pervading, massless medium hypothesized by archaic physics as the force that propagates the electromagnetic fields that radiate through and energize the universe. Nearby, a great pseudo-electromagnet is poised as if to activate the ether wind. Aycock's deliberate use of an erroneous concept both parallels Robert Fludd's indifference to the growing rationalism of his time and, more significantly, evokes the unfathomable mystery of the source of energy in the universe. Fludd believed that the creation was generated as God first withdrew himself from part of the firmament and then reentered the void to become the creation. In *Hoodo,* the whirling shape that generates the ether wind must count as the unending source of sources.

Juxtaposed with the central source is the second element of *Hoodo*: a series of large metal rings of various sizes hung from a horizontal axis which turns them. They are essentially a schematic representation of the vertically oriented central engine, and serve as a kind of "index" or annotation to the main form.

The third major element Aycock calls "the big twist"; its physical form is a long, undulating ribbon of sheet metal which forms a large elliptical segment that courses round the whirling "mother image." The break in the ellipse is, as Aycock describes it, "for catching ghosts," by which she means the vital plasmic energy radiating from the source. Across the room, a large, empty, harness-like device awaiting a bearer repeats the theme of catching and harnessing the intangible force. Aycock's ghosts, from *The Series Entitled "How to Catch and Man-*

ufacture Ghosts," are another manifestation of the elusive and terrible energy that takes the form here of ether wind. (*'Hoodo'* is a colloquialism for a ghost and thus a fitting title for this work, itself a single incarnation of the infinite creative power.)

From Aycock's earliest days as an artist, her work has been an attempt to catch and manufacture intangible, elusive, fleeting realities. It is as if she were after some animate life-force which she knows to be always afoot somewhere in the universe but can only glimpse momentarily and peripherally. For example, her 1971 *Cloud Piece* (one of her earliest published works[2]) documented the formation, movement, and dissipation of cumulus clouds as photographed sequentially by a stationary camera. Since then, first in her wood constructions and now through her comparatively "high-tech" machines, she has pursued this animate force in such states (as named in the titles of her works) as memories, desire, ghosts, angels, and the ether wind, representing them with fire, caged birds, heat, and light. Yet, as Aycock acknowledges, her machines, for all their imagery of robust power, are incapable of delivering the ghosts and angels and magic promised in their conjuring titles. Aycock recognizes this as their destiny, a function of their ontological condition as mere matter, as clumsy mechanisms.

In this there is a subtle anthropomorphism to Aycock's machines, a tragicomic aspect reinforced by their corporeality: these unwieldy hulks suggest energy and exertion and are prone to breakdowns due to overexertion and imperfect qualities that leave them stranded in their would-be purposes. Aycock's machines get progressively more complex, more sophisticated, yet they remain mere approximations, chimeras of that force of which they partake and which they are said to represent. With us, they inhabit a shadow world and are the detritus of the force that animates them. At the least they are artifice; at best they inspire a wonderment at the unknown forces that organize the universe. And if the only real force that organizes them is the imagination of the artist, then they bespeak Aycock's almost sacramental optimism, her supremely Romantic vision that man's redemption and the joy of his desiring lie in art.

Detail of *Hoodo (Laura)*

Notes

1. Donald B. Kuspit, "Aycock's Dream Houses," *Art in America* 68 (September 1980): 86.
2. Illustrated in Lucy R. Lippard, *Six Years: The Dematerialization of the Art Object from 1966 to 1972* (New York: Praeger Publishers, 1973), p. 253.

Lauren Ewing

Born in Fort Knox, Kentucky, October 13, 1946.
Lives in New York.

Education

B.A., Skidmore College, Saratoga Springs, New York, 1968.

M.A., Indiana State University, Terre Haute, 1971.

M.F.A., University of California, Santa Barbara, 1973.

Awards

National Endowment for the Arts Artists Fellowship, 1980.

Selected Solo Exhibitions

University Gallery, University of California, Santa Barbara, 1972.

North Gallery, University of California, Santa Barbara, 1973.

Gallery 9, Williams College Museum, Williamstown, Massachusetts, 1974.

Artists Space, New York, 1975.

P.S.1, Institute for Art and Urban Resources, New York, 1979.

Skidmore College, Saratoga Springs, New York, 1981.

Selected Group Exhibitions

25 to 2000: An Event of Conceptual Art, N.A.M.E. Gallery, Chicago, 1975.

Statements/Architecture, Louisiana University, School of Art and Architecture, Ruston, Louisiana, 1979.

Artists' Prints, Grey Art Gallery, New York University, New York, and tour 1979.

Marking Black, Bronx Museum of the Arts, New York, 1980.

Sculpture 1980, Maryland Institute, College of Art, Baltimore, 1980.

Investigations: Probe, Structure, Analysis, The New Museum, New York, 1980.

Architectural Sculpture, Los Angeles Institute of Contemporary Art, 1980.

Installation '81, Rhode Island School of Design, Providence, 1981.

Windows, Chase Manhattan Bank, New York, 1981.

Artists Make Architecture, Rosa Esman Gallery, New York, 1981.

Schemes: A Decade of Installation Drawings, Elise Meyer Gallery, New York, and tour, 1981–82.

Art on the Beach, Battery Park Landfill, New York, 1981.

Selected Bibliography

Burnside, Madeleine, and Ingberman, Jeanette. *Marking Black,* exhibition catalog. New York: Bronx Museum of the Arts, 1980.

Coplan, Robin. *Sculpture '80,* exhibition catalog. Baltimore: Maryland Institute, College of Art and the City of Baltimore, 1980.

Gray, Channing. "She Draws on Her Experience." *Providence* (R.I.) *Journal,* January 25, 1981, p. H10.

Gurchiek, Kathy. "Environmental Sculpture 'Fanciful' Says Artist." *Terre Haute* (Ind.) *Tribune Star,* February 15, 1981, sec. E, p. 6.

Larson, Kay. "Artists the Critics Are Watching: Lauren Ewing: Setting Her Sites on Power." *Art News* 80 (May 1981): 78–79.

———. "Dinner Belles." *Village Voice,* October 22–28, 1980, p. 77.

———. "Reports from the Front." *Village Voice,* July 2–8, 1980, p. 60.

Lippard, Lucy R. *From the Center: Feminist Essays on Women's Art,* p. 133. New York: E. P. Dutton and Co., 1976.

Schwartzman, Allan, and Gumpert, Lynn. *Investigations: Probe, Structure, Analysis: Agnes Denes, Lauren Ewing, Vernon Fisher, Stephen Prina, David Reed,* exhibition catalog, pp. 12–14, 24–27, 42. New York: New Museum, 1980.

Vaterlaus, Eve, and Waltemath, Joan. *Space Window,* exhibition catalog. Providence: Providence Inner City Arts Association and Rhode Island State Council for the Arts, 1977.

Wortz, Melinda. "University of California, Irvine." In *Architectural Sculpture: Projects,* exhibition catalog, pp. 38–41, 43, 50–51. Los Angeles: Los Angeles Institute of Contemporary Art, 1980.

Zimmer, William. "Art 1: Beached." *Soho News,* July 15–21, 1981, p. 41.

QUANTA: Last Night I Dreamed I Saw a Strong Blind Man Carrying a Sighted Cripple on His Back. They Were Searching for a Key to the Fields, 1980
Installation at Pier #1, Baltimore Inner Harbor
Wood
2.7 × 7.2 × 3.6 (9 × 24 × 12)

The structure can be entered in a crouched position by the spectator/viewer, who has a view of the cityscape and harbor but is very much enclosed by the body/structure. The structure faces a prototype industrial building across the harbor which generated the form of the smaller structure. Marked by the word QUANTA, *which means a discrete measure of energy, the smaller structure contains an analogue of the science/industry controversy and contains within it the capacity to question unquestioned progress by the introduction of the characters of two handicapped travelers who are in search of some "mythic key."*
—Lauren Ewing

The Library: A Device for Storing the Winds of the World (Before and After the Famous Random Event), 1981
Installation at Skidmore College, Saratoga Springs, New York
Wood and steel construction with video installation
4.1 × 5.5 × 5.5 (13½ × 18 × 18)

Inscription:
THE LIBRARY: A DEVICE FOR / STORING THE WINDS OF THE / WORLD (BEFORE AND AFTER / THE FAMOUS RANDOM EVENT)

Each pediment is topped with a small sphere bearing the names of four famous libraries. The video text, the luminous word, further elucidates the theme of The Library. *The text deals with aspects of the mind/library storage, infinite retrieval, private and social memory, linkage, item velocity, total recall, etc.* The Library *is encyclopedic and referential, haunted by a vast and instantly available past. Its simulation of historic modes provokes associations and also opens possibilities for the generation of further eccentric taxonomies and accumulations for the future.* The Library *is a post-modern device.*
—Lauren Ewing

A Powerhouse for Adam Smith, 1980
Installation at The New Museum, New York
Wood construction with audiovisual installation
4.4 × 4.8 × 2.4 (14½ × 16 × 8)

Inscriptions:
THE BUILDING/MACHINE, SUGAR CUBE, TRICKSTER, DOPPELGÄNGER
A POWERHOUSE FOR ADAM SMITH
LIAR, LIAR, FANCIFIER, YOU WHEEL SPINNER, TOWER AND WELL . . . (LATER DESCRIBED AS CONTAGION)

The Powerhouse: A Device for Gaining Heart, 1981
Installation at Rhode Island School of Design, Providence
Wood construction with audiovisual installation
4.7 × 4.8 × 2.4 (15½ × 16 × 8)

Inscriptions:
THE POWERHOUSE
AN ENERGY GAIN SECTOR (ATTEMPTING TO FALL OUTSIDE THE REVERSIBILITY OF SIGNS OR POWER AND DOMINATION)
A CONSPIRACY, A FAKE, A RERUN, SIMULATION
A DEVICE FOR GAINING HEART

As the viewer approaches, his/her voice and movements are picked up by a sensitive microphone and projected inside the powerhouse. A video monitor uses both image and text to further conflate the situation. The text on the screen begins

WITNESS
THE OLD WORLD VIEW
APPARENT CONCRETENESS
CRYSTALLIZATIONS OF POWER
VALUE ASSIGNMENTS

and suddenly addresses itself to THE NEW SCIENCE. The remainder of the video text elucidates the content of THE NEW SCIENCE, which—in short—is "autonomy." This is a post-political, non-partisan, non-ideological text which touches on aspects of individual power and enlightenment. It ends

INSTINCTUAL TRIGGERS
LIGHT THE LAMP
THAT RADICAL AND ORIGINAL DREAM
THE BODY BREATHES ITSELF
—Lauren Ewing

Auto-Plastique: The Prison, 1981
Installation at Hirshhorn Museum and Sculpture Garden
Painted wood construction, megaphone, and paint on existing gallery wall
Overall dimensions of site approx. 8.5 × 10.7 (28 × 35)

Even in the company of works as demanding as the other five projects in this exhibition, Lauren Ewing's *Auto-Plastique: The Prison* stands out by virtue of the stark, nearly impassive theatricality of its challenge. If the other artists court our imaginations with stunning apocalyptic images, straightforward invitations for physical participation, and hypnotically furious interaction of moving parts, Ewing seems almost to dare us to investigate the mysteries of her eerie Kafkaesque landscape.

Ewing's sculptures are condensed-scale architectural representations painted a light-absorbing matte black. They are characteristically modeled after large public buildings such as factories, powerhouses, and libraries, generic architectural types that reflect the values and accomplishments of complex, economically developed societies. The artist focuses on the symbolic roles of such buildings in the systems created by technologically advanced cultures in order to pursue their aspirations and safeguard their welfare.

Without disavowing the obvious societal implications of her structures, Ewing has made it clear that she intends them also as metaphors for the mind. She has described them as dealing with "vision," the intellectual and intuitive perceptions by which we identify ourselves and external reality, and "power," the emotional, rational, and physical transactions through which we act on these perceptions to establish concrete functioning relationships with the outside world. By exercising vision and power in tandem, we develop, and constantly revise, a sense of our own possibilities, a kind of self-socialization that Ewing calls "infrapsychic molding."

The Prison is one of a suite of six projects,[1] all of them realized or in an advanced planning stage, based on institutional architecture; together they are meant to embody the full range of forces which mold society and, by extension, the analogous forces which shape the individual. In Ewing's rather idiosyncratic universe, the first three institutions represented in this suite—a powerhouse, a library, and a bank—are ones in which we voluntarily participate for the bounty, energy, nurture, and knowledge they provide. The second three—a school, an asylum, and a prison—are institutions of regimentation, confinement, and surveillance in which we participate against our will.

The Prison is presented as a kind of austere outsized stage set composed of three freestanding architectural elements. The dominant structure is an unlabeled cellblcok of seven compartments or cells forming a segmented arc approximately eight feet high and twenty-four feet across. This structure has no doors, but the tiers of windows which deck its walls reveal the interior of each of the seven cells to contain a writing desk and a stool, both of them exaggeratedly tall and narrow. A cylindrical guard tower, bearing the legend "The Prison," is centered in front of the semicircular core of the cellblock, creating the ominous surveillance zone which characterized English utilitarian philosopher Jeremy Bentham's proposed "panopticon" prison design. Situated slightly behind and to one side of the guard tower is a triangular kiosk, with two walls facing the center of the prison complex and the third side open. Mounted into the front of this booth, which is labeled "The Perfect Speaker," is the brilliant red shape of a loudspeaker. Connected to this speaker from the other side of the wall is a pipe which ends in a flared mouthpiece accessible from the open side of the booth. Painted high on the gallery wall facing the complex is the outline of a megaphone with "Auto" printed along its side and "Glaz" in the elliptical opening. Below this image, and much larger, is a tapered rendering of the word "Plastique."

Initially *The Prison* may appear to be little more than an object-bound melodrama, a strikingly depicted but simple notation on the dynamics of authority, transgression, and punishment. Moving through its enigmatic landscape, however, the viewer encounters a series of elements and relationships among elements which bespeak a far more complex and cerebral content. The title of the work alone summons a variety of images. "Auto-plastique" translates literally as "self-molding"; in conjunction with "The Prison," it raises the issue of a social covenant in which we voluntarily participate out of general self-interest in spite of the possibility that it may at some time coercively limit our freedom to act. The combination also suggests "auto-da-fé" (the pronouncement and execution of sentence by that archetypically self-righteous and merciless authority, the Inquisition) and the dramatically contrasting notion of "autoplasty" (the surgical repair of a malfunctioning body by a graft of tissue from elsewhere on that body). When "auto-plastique" is broken into its discrete elements, as it is in the wall graphic, additional nuances come into play. "Auto," as a prefix connoting direction from within, echoes Ewing's "infrapsychic dialogue" concept, while "plastique" refers both to a dance technique of frozen or slowly altering poses and to plastic explosives, conveniently malleable but destructive.

Other elements of language displayed in this project—and their specific locations—contribute additional dimensions to its conceptual operation. The legend "The Prison," appearing as it does on the guard tower rather than the cellblock, suggests that authority in some way confines itself more profoundly than it does those who violate its dictates. The exalted title "Perfect Speaker" is given to the least imposing of the three architectural elements in this piece. Indeed, whatever promise of infallible reason and wisdom we may perceive in this entity ultimately proves aprocryphal: the speaker is capable of emitting only silence or the presumably irrelevant utterings of someone who, by positioning himself at the mouthpiece, has no possible views or knowledge of the prison universe.

"Reciprocal vision," the notion that two people see each other with equal clarity, is—in Ewing's view of interpersonal relations—a function of mutual interest and good will; where vision is not feasibly reciprocal, something is ethically or psychologically wrong. The idea of internal vision is implicit in the images painted on the gallery wall. The combination of "auto" and "glaz" (a transliteration of the Russian word for "eye"), appearing as they do on a megaphone and above all other elements in the project, suggests that introspective vision somehow "speaks" more truly, significantly, and productively than does our perceptual relationship with the outside world.

Metaphorically, the three-part anatomy of the prison complex parallels the tripartite topography of the psyche proposed by Sigmund Freud, with the inward-curving cellblock symbolizing the instinctive, gratification-seeking id; the guard tower acting as the conscious, eternal reality-responsive ego; and the "Perfect Speaker" representing the superego, struggling to reconcile the conflicting impulses of the other two and rendered permanently silent by the impossibility of its task. The conceptual working of *The Prison,* as a reflection of both individual and societal "self-molding," is further enriched by the "panopticon" configuration of the project. While its surveillance zone does smack of punitive incarceration and deprivation of privacy and autonomy, this prison design is actually the product of Jeremy Bentham's progressive view that, beyond the immediate protection of society, the proper objective of imprisonment is not punishment but rehabilitation. His vision of "morals reformed, health preserved, industry invigorated [he advocated useful work instead of hard labor for prisoners], instruction diffused" is reflected conceptually in the sense of "autoplasty" and visually in the instruments of study housed in the cellblock.

It should be noted here that Ewing's previous projects have included amplified audio effects, video presentations, and displays of relatively extensive text in addition to architectural forms; by comparison, *Auto-Plastique: The Prison* seems stripped down, severe, literally understated. Even in its physical simplicity, however, it replicates the definitive experiential/reflective operation of metaphorical art: the viewer's senses are engaged through theatrical presentation of a very few sculptural and linguistic elements whose disjunctive and synthetic interplay conjures up a profusion of thematically related but conflicting ideas which, in turn, engage the viewer's intellect. Content is potentially rich but inexact; in Ewing's

Auto-Plastique: The Prison

words, it "defies specific location." It resides in the tensions among conceptual images, the evocation of which constitutes her art.

Note

1. In addition to *Auto-Plastique: The Prison,* this suite consists of *The Bank: Opus Proprium*; *The Powerhouse: A Device for Gaining Heart*; *The Library: A Device for Storing the Winds of the World (Before and After the Famous Random Event)*; *The Asylum*; and *The School: William, James, Walt, Clover, Alice, Margaret.*

Detail of *Auto-Plastique: The Prison*

Robert Morris

Born in Kansas City, Missouri, February 9, 1931.
Lives in New York.

Bevan Davies

Detail of *Preludes (for A.B.): Roller Disco: Cenotaph for a Public Figure,* 1980

Education

M.F.A., Hunter College, New York City, 1966.

Awards

John Simon Guggenheim Memorial Foundation Fellowship, 1969.

Selected Solo Exhibitions

Dilexi Gallery, San Francisco, 1957–58.

Green Gallery, New York, 1963–65.

Leo Castelli Gallery, New York, from 1967.

Galerie Ileana Sonnabend, Paris, and Sonnabend Gallery, New York, from 1968.

Stedelijk van Abbemuseum, Eindhoven, The Netherlands, 1968.

Corcoran Gallery of Art, Washington, D.C., 1969, and The Detroit Institute of Arts, 1970.

Whitney Museum of American Art, New York, 1970.

Tate Gallery, London, 1971.

Institute of Contemporary Art, University of Pennsylvania, Philadelphia, 1974.

Contemporary Arts Museum, Houston, 1981.

Selected Group Exhibitions

Primary Structures, Jewish Museum, New York, 1966.

Annual Exhibition, Whitney Museum of American Art, New York, 1966, 1968, 1970; *Biennial Exhibition,* 1973.

American Sculpture of the Sixties, Los Angeles County Museum of Art and Philadelphia Museum of Art, 1967.

5th Guggenheim International Exhibition, Solomon R. Guggenheim Museum, New York, 1967; 6th, 1971.

Earthworks, Dwan Gallery, New York, 1968.

Minimal Art, Gemeentemuseum, The Hague, 1968.

The Art of the Real: USA 1948–1968, The Museum of Modern Art, New York, and tour, 1968–69.

14 Sculptors: The Industrial Edge, Walker Art Center, Minneapolis, 1969.

Anti-Illusion: Procedures/Materials, Whitney Museum of American Art, New York, 1969.

New York Painting and Sculpture: 1940–1970, Metropolitan Museum of Art, New York, 1969–70.

Spaces, The Museum of Modern Art, New York, 1970.

Preludes (for A.B.), 1980
Installation at Sonnabend Gallery, New York, 1980
Italian onyx, silkscreened text, lights, metal, plastic, installed with black paint
Onyx pieces variable, each approximately .9 × .9 × .15 (3 × 3 × ½)

Bevan Davies

Information, The Museum of Modern Art, New York, 1970.

Art in Landscape, traveling exhibition organized by Independent Curators, Inc., Washington, D.C., 1975.

Documenta VI, Kassel, West Germany, 1977.

Probing the Earth: Contemporary Land Projects, Hirshhorn Museum and Sculpture Garden, Washington, D.C., 1977–78, and tour, 1978.

Morris, Acconci, Oppenheim, Sonnabend Gallery, New York, 1980.

Summer Group Show, Sonnabend Gallery, New York, 1981.

Westkunst: Zeitgenössische Kunst seit 1939, Museen der Stadt Köln, West Germany, 1981.

Selected Bibliography

Antin, David. "Art and Information, 1: Grey Paint, Robert Morris." *Art News* 65 (April 1966): 22–24, 56–58.

Beardsley, John. *Probing the Earth: Contemporary Land Projects,* exhibition catalog. Washington, D.C.: Smithsonian Institution Press for Hirshhorn Museum and Sculpture Garden, 1977.

Burnham, Jack. "Robert Morris: Retrospective in Detroit." *Artforum* 8 (March 1970): 67–75.

Calas, Nicolas. "Wit and Pedantry of Robert Morris." *Arts Magazine* 44 (March 1970): 44–47.

Compton, Michael, and Sylvester, David. *Robert Morris,* exhibition catalog. London: Tate Gallery, 1971.

Eisenman, Stephen F. "The Space of the Self: Robert Morris' 'In the Realm of the Carceral.' " *Arts Magazine* 55 (September 1980): 104-9.

Fineberg, Jonathan. "Robert Morris Looking Back: An Interview." *Arts Magazine* 55 (September 1980): 110–15.

Fried, Michael. "Art and Objecthood." *Artforum* 5 (Summer 1967): 12–23. Reprinted in *Minimal Art: A Critical Anthology,* edited by Gregory Battcock, pp. 116–47. New York: E. P. Dutton & Co., 1968.

Fry, Edward F. "Robert Morris: The Dialectic." *Arts Magazine* 49 (September 1974): 22–24.

———. *Robert Morris: Grand Rapids Project,* exhibition catalog. Grand Rapids: Grand Rapids Art Museum, 1975.

Glozer, Laszlo. *Westkunst: Zeitgenössische Kunst seit 1939,* exhibition catalog. Cologne: DuMont Buchverlag, 1981.

Goossen, E. C. "The Artist Speaks: Robert Morris." *Art in America* 58 (May–June 1970): 104–11.

Henri, Adrian. *Total Art: Environments, Happenings, and Performances.* New York: Praeger Publishers, 1974.

Herman, Jerry. "Arts Reviews: 3 Installations: Sonnabend." *Arts Magazine* 54 (June 1980): 33–34.

Kardon, Janet. *Time,* exhibition catalog, p. 40. Philadelphia: Philadelphia College of Art, 1977.

Kozloff, Max. "The Division and Mockery of the Self." *Studio International* 179 (January 1970): 9–15.

Krauss, Rosalind E. *Passages in Modern Sculpture.* New York: Viking Press, 1977.

———. "Sense and Sensibility: Reflection on Post '60s Sculpture." *Artforum* 12 (November 1973): 43–52.

Kuspit, Donald B. "The Artist (Neo-Dandy) Stripped Bare by His Critic (Neo-Careerist), Almost." *Arts Magazine* 54 (May 1980): 134–37.

Larson, Kay "Metaphysical Attraction." *Village Voice,* March 17, 1980, p. 79.

Lippard, Lucy R. *Six Years: The Dematerialization of the Art Object from 1966 to 1972.* New York: Praeger Publishers, 1973.

Bevan Davies

Second Study for a View from a Corner of Orion (Day), 1980
Installation at Leo Castelli Gallery, New York
Steel, aluminum, mirror, human bones, silver leaf
3.1 × 3.7 × 4.9 (10 × 32 × 16)

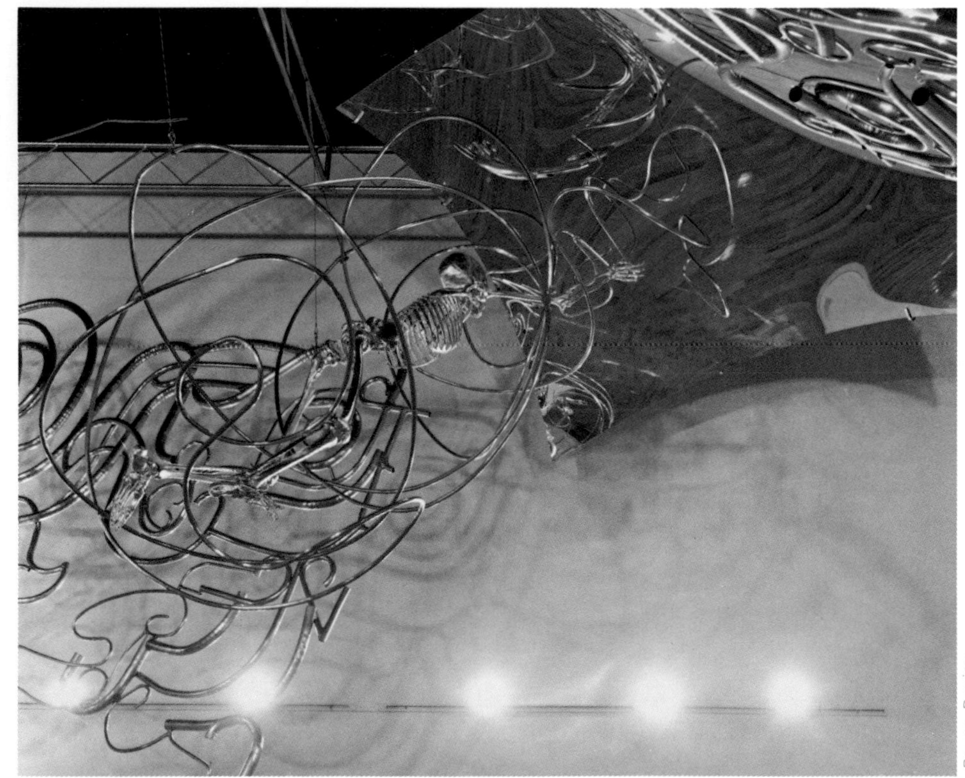
Bevan Davies

Detail of *Second Study for a View from a Corner of Orion (Day)*, 1980

McShine, Kynaston. *Primary Structures: Younger American and British Sculptors,* exhibition catalog. New York: Jewish Museum, 1966.

Mayo, Marti. *Robert Morris: Selected Works 1970–1980,* exhibition catalog. Houston: Contemporary Arts Museum, 1981. Documentation by Patrick J. Ladden.

Michelson, Annette. *Robert Morris,* exhibition catalog. Washington, D.C.: Corcoran Gallery of Art, 1969.

Morris, Robert. "Aligned with Nazca." *Artforum* 14 (October 1975): 26–39.

———. "Cold Oracle." *Tracks* 2 (Fall 1976): 47–52.

———. [Installation photographs and text of cenotaphs in *Preludes (for A. B.),* Sonnabend Gallery, New York, 1980]. *Chelsea* 39 (1980): 99–112.

———. "Notes on Sculpture," part 1. *Artforum* 4 (February 1966): 42–44. Part 2, *Artforum* 5 (October 1966): 20–23. Part 3, *Artforum* 5 (Summer 1967): 24–29. "Beyond Objects," part 4, *Artforum* 7 (April 1969): 50–54.

———. "The Present Tense of Space." *Art in America* 66 (January–February 1978): 70–81.

———. *Robert Morris: Mirror Works 1961–78,* exhibition catalog. New York: Leo Castelli, 1979.

———. "Some Notes on the Phenomenology of Making: The Search for the Motivated." *Artforum* 8 (April 1970): 62–66.

Nasgaard, Roald. *Structures for Behavior: New Sculptures by Robert Morris, David Rabinowitch, Richard Serra and George Trakas,* exhibition catalog. Toronto: Art Gallery of Ontario, 1978.

Ratcliff, Carter. "Robert Morris: Prisoner of Modernism." *Art in America* 67 (October 1979): 96–109.

Rose, Barbara. "ABC Art." *Art in America* 53 (October–November 1965): 57–69.

Shapiro, David. "Mr. Processionary at the Conceptacle." *Art News* 69 (September 1970): 58–61.

Staniszewski, Mary Anne. "New York Reviews: Acconci, Morris, Oppenheim (Sonnabend)." *Art News* 79 (September 1980): 248–49.

Tucker, Marcia. *Robert Morris,* exhibition catalog, New York: Whitney Museum of American Art, 1970.

Jornada del Muerto (from "The Natural History of Los Alamos"), 1981
Installation at Hirshhorn Museum and Sculpture Garden
Nylon, felt, paint, photomechanical reproduction, mirrors, steel, human skeletons
Overall dimensions of site approx. 8.5 × 10.7 (28 × 35)

No case is more paradigmatic of the progression from Modern to post-Modern art than that of Robert Morris: the development of his oeuvre from strict formalist orthodoxy into some of the most provocative and imaginative expressions of metaphorical art reads as a condensation of the art history of the period.

In the late 1960s Morris stood as one of the foremost practitioners of Minimal sculpture, with its emphasis on elemental geometric forms essentially devoid of anthropomorphic content. He was acknowledged as one of the then-new art's most articulate apologists as well. Working within an awesomely restrictive canon of formal options and perceptual mechanics, Morris produced a major body of supremely reductive, literalist sculpture, the content of which was limited to what could be empirically confirmed from his exploration and exploitation of sculptural forms.[1]

From about 1968 and through the '70s, however, Morris explored various options that broke with the formal aesthetic of the object in space, executing a succession of bodies of work that are best described as antiformal: large expanses of thick felt drooping from the wall or spilling in strips onto the floor; heaps of felt strips, rubber, clumps of threadwaste, and assorted shapes of metal, stone, or wood, all scattered in apparently random masses about the floor; earthworks and land projects for indoor or outdoor sites; and mirror works whose surfaces became progressively more convoluted, drastically distorting reflected space. The literalism and militant empiricism of Morris's Minimalist works thus gradually eroded until it became difficult to discern just what comprised the sculptural forms of Morris's spatially oriented works—even to determine where they stopped and their surroundings began. As his projects became indefinite or even indeterminate in form, they came more and more to suggest spaces and things known empirically *not* to be present and to provoke imaginative, rather than simply perceptual, responses. A 1979 statement by Morris about his longtime use of mirrors in his sculpture illuminates this development: "In the beginning I was ambivalent about its [the mirror's] fraudulent space, its blatant illusionism. Later its very suspiciousness seemed a virtue."[2] The mirror created what Morris has called a "mental space"[3]—a metaphorical space, artificially generated, that exists in or is a projection of the imagination and is an analogue of the real world. Morris's statement reflects the pronounced evolutional shift of his work away from such exclusively literal and materialistic object-bound concerns as light, space, shape, proportion, size, or surface, to an art of ambiguity, suspicions, and imaginative evocations.

In 1980 Morris produced a disturbing work, anomalous even within his notably varied oeuvre; *Preludes (for A.B.)* was a highly theatrical installation that consisted of ominously glowing cenotaphs (sepulchral monuments to the memory of deceased persons buried elsewhere) arranged at eye level along the walls of a darkened room, each topped with a death's head. Those commemorated in this theater of death were the imagined villains and victims in the piecemeal destruction of the habitable world by such forces as chemical and industrial poisoning, economic imperialism, and materialistic decadence. Although the flagrantly literary content of this political memento mori confounded or dismayed many of Morris's observers, it established the direction he has pursued in his work since.

The "A.B." of that sardonic prelude (actually the initials of the friend to whom it was dedicated) might appropriately have referred to the atomic bomb that is the subject of *Jornada del Muerto,* the project Morris conceived for this exhibition. It is from the series Morris has titled *The Natural History of Los Alamos* that deals with the destruction of the world. Los Alamos, of course, is the city that was built beginning in 1939 in the emptiness of the New Mexican desert for the purpose of developing the atomic bomb; Jornada del Muerto, which means journey, or day's journey, or a day's work of death, is the traditional name of the parched desert valley south of Los Alamos where the bomb was first tested.

Jornada del Muerto begins in darkness, as the viewer encounters a curtain of thick black felt hanging at an entryway recessed just deeply enough into the gallery to beckon the viewer into the ominous space beyond. Within this space an apocalyptic vision—a riot of deadly images of ultimate destruction—erupts into view. Suspended at eye level on brackets about a foot out from the three walls of the room are a series of large photographic montages depicting the history of the atomic bomb from its assembly at Los Alamos to the wreckage and burn victims of Hiroshima. On the wall directly behind each panel is a flat mirror in which is reflected one of Leonardo da Vinci's drawings of the deluge. Each of these double "tablets" of divine and human destructiveness is crowned by a grimacing black skull. In the center of the room, arranged in an arc and facing the fourth wall of the gallery, stand four severely contorted mirrors, at once symbols and instruments of both vanity and truth, hideously deforming the reflected space. They are trained on the gruesome centerpiece of *Jornada del Muerto:* in the background looms a stark black-and-white appliquéd mural whose stylized form depicts the distinctive mushroom cloud of the atomic blast, as viewed from so near Ground Zero that annihilation of the viewer is imminent. Bursting forth from this nuclear holocaust and suspended from the ceiling are four missiles, each ridden by a black-painted human skeleton—the nuclear age's Four Horsemen of the Apocalypse, come to wreak their chaos and vengeance on the world, careening into this ruptured, distorted stage set of death. Around the periphery of the space, just below the ceiling, hover stylized images of a thunderbird and other Hopi Indian motifs, ironic reminders of the once noble civilizations ("Hopi" means "peaceful" in the Hopi language) that inhabited the Americas. At the exit of this grim pageant two large flags of thick black felt with three-dimensional stars and stripes hang leadenly against a wall.

The tradition of apocalyptic art in the Western world is a long one. Religious and secular visions of the end of the world range from the apocalyptic frescoes of Cimabue, through Albrecht Dürer's famous woodcuts of the Four Horsemen, to Leonardo's drawings of the deluge, Michelangelo's Sistine Chapel frescoes of *The Last Judgment,* and Pablo Picasso's allegorical *Guernica*—a masterwork which also reflects the related artistic tradition of depictions of warfare, massacre, slaughter, and final conflict. *Jornada del Muerto* plainly aligns itself with these related traditions in Western art to create a harrowing spectacle of a nuclear Armageddon.

Robert Morris has a history of political activism, but only recently have his political convictions begun to manifest themselves so overtly in his work. *Jornada del Muerto's* strident political statement must be understood as an act of conscience. This remarkable tour de force explicitly declares Morris's profound concern (and what he would deem a societal guilt in which all share) for the creation of the atomic bomb and its horrible effects, and represents his deepest protest against its continued development and possible deployment.

To discount in any way the emphatic moralizing which constitutes the new element in Morris's recent works would be unquestionably remiss. Yet these recent projects also partake of both a *behavioral* element explicit in much of Morris's previous work and a *metaphysical* dimension that has been implicit in his art from the outset. In this regard these highly theatrical installations reveal themselves to be less radical departures from his persistent concerns than they may at first seem. Morris has long contended that experiencing his works involves not mere passive observation but active behavior. Among his earliest works, for example, were a number of movable sculptures that were used as props in dance performances; his later Minimal structures engaged the viewer's perceptual and physical activity alike; and his subsequent mazes and convoluted mirror works also required active viewer participation. In the light of Morris's oft-stated intention to engage the viewer's perceptual and physical behavior in his work, it is not surprising that he

Detail of *Jornada del Muerto*

Detail of *Jornada del Muerto*

Detail of *Jornada del Muerto*

has been moved to address the viewer's political and ethical behavior as well. Indeed, considering also the evolution of his oeuvre, away from object-bound literalist concerns to a preoccupation with what may be implied by an object's very artifice, such a development seems only inevitable. Moreover, the use of art to instruct or to advance a moral position is one of the most venerable and ancient of artistic traditions, considerably pre-dating Aristotle's early and persuasive argument for the morality of art; Aristotle's teachings, like the Greek culture they commented upon, are well known to Morris, and he clearly has embraced the moral imperative in his recent art.

Behavioral import and political content notwithstanding, the metaphysical dimension so apprehensible in *Preludes (for A.B.)* and *Jornada del Muerto* has been a latent presence in all of Morris's work. Throughout his oeuvre, Morris has persistently explored the relationship between what is seen and what is not seen; between what is overt and what is implied; between immediate physical perception and cognitive reflection. His thoughts on these relationships surface repeatedly in his writings, but they are most fully articulated in his rigorous essay "The Present Tense of Space,"[4] which, while ostensibly not about Morris's own work, illuminates his principal aesthetic concerns. In that article Morris outlines, with references to both historical precedents and contemporary examples, a fundamental distinction between three-dimensional art, which engages the viewer's active participation through time and space, and that which presents itself as a static form perceived optically. Morris finds the more active experience of "presentness" to be, if not necessarily a more advanced state, certainly a fundamental and vital one that was conspicuously alien to much Modern art. His implied conclusion, that a truly heightened consciousness of art experience must embrace both modes, seems to characterize much of what may be described as post-Modern art.

This rather mechanical polarity that is Morris's subject has a metaphysical analogue, however, one which may well point to a dimension of content not often remarked on in Morris's art. In detailing his model of the experience of "presentness," and its distinction from the experience of other properties in art, Morris subscribed to American philosopher George Herbert Mead's suggestion of a parallel or correlative dichotomy between two modes of the self: the "I" and the "me"—modes which Morris associates respectively with the sensate, moving, immediately experiential self and the cognitive, static, recollective self.

This dichotomous self has further associations and ramifications in the experience of Morris's work. The "I" is temporally and spatially oriented, corporeal, sensual, and responsive immediately to external conditions; while the "me" is timeless, disembodied, immaterial, and cerebral, responsive to language, memory, and reflection. To a remarkable degree this dichotomy virtually recapitulates the Platonic scheme of the duality of the real and the ideal, of the experience and its meaning, of the act and its morality—and by extension, the duality of body and soul. This dichotomy and its concomitant recognition of the dual nature of selfhood and of the art experience have persisted throughout Morris's oeuvre.

No other modern sculptor, it seems, has been quite so consistently and profoundly concerned with the relationship of body and soul as has Robert Morris. In *Jornada del Muerto* he has created a highly theatrical, fantastic space—what Morris would describe as "a material metaphor for mental space which is in turn the 'me's' metaphor for the space of the world"[5]—as well as a "present-tense" space, ambiguous but real, in whose presence the viewer's activity and explorations are engaged. *Jornada del Muerto* involves the viewer's whole being—"I" and "me," physical and mental, body and soul. It is a dramatic irony that this fullness of selfhood is addressed so cogently in Morris's tragic portent of the ultimate dissociation of body and soul, a dark vision, not just of the death of the individual, but of the annihilation of humankind.

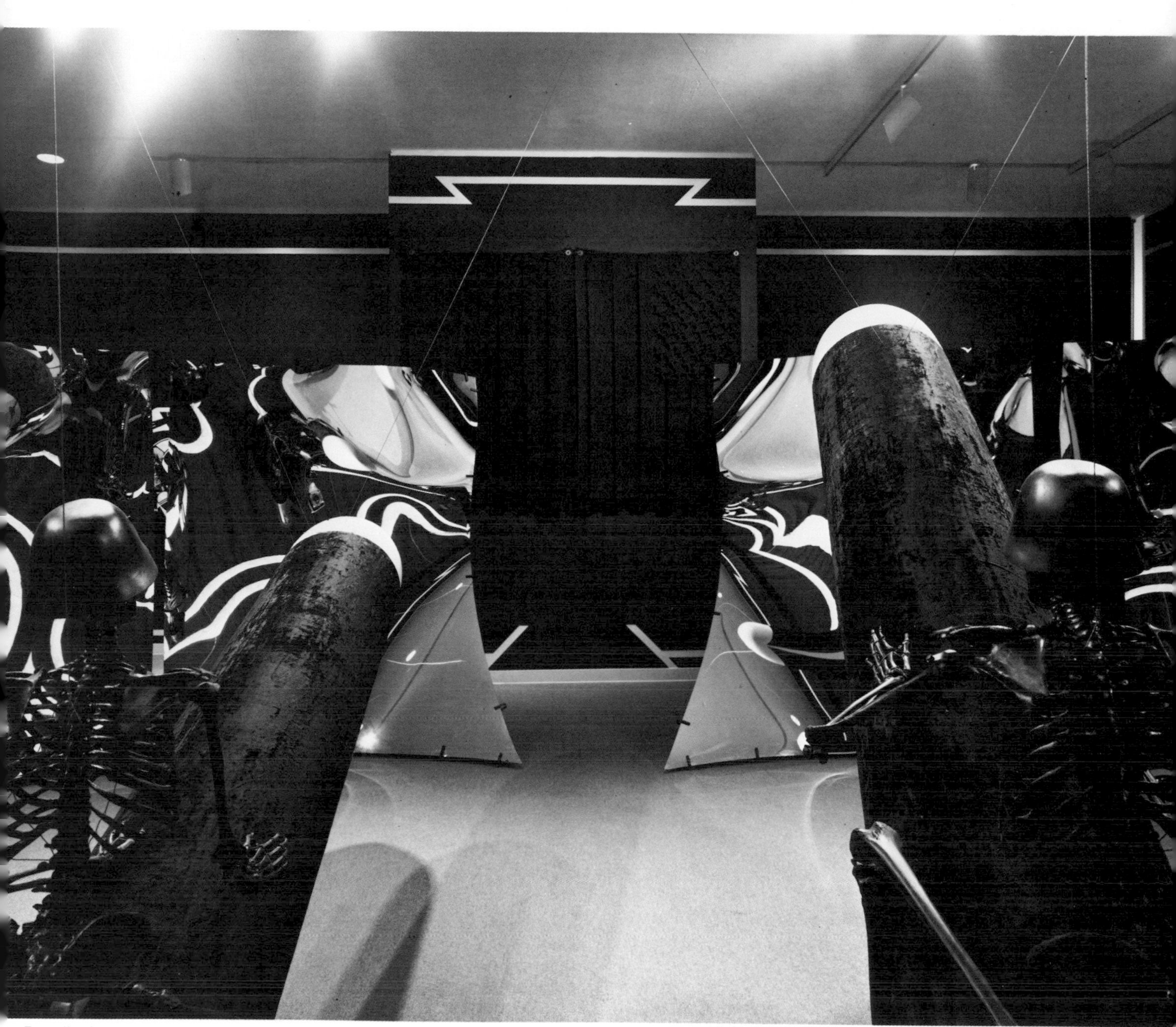

Detail of *Jornada del Muerto*

Notes

1. Morris has always contended that the temporal and spatial aspects involved in experiencing his early work separated it from the Modern aesthetic that was launched by Cubism, explaining in various statements that his intention was "diametrically opposed to Cubism with its concern for simultaneous views in one plane," and that in his view the Minimal aesthetic was qualitatively different from the Cubist (i.e., Modernist) aesthetic, "in which what is to be had from the work is located strictly within the specific object." Morris seems in such statements clearly intent on placing his art somewhere *beyond* Modernism. Yet his recitation of the variables that typically would conspire to affect the experience of his Minimalist work—"light, space, . . . shaping, proportions, size, surface"—are precisely the formal ingredients that had been the basis of Modernist art through the twentieth century; and Morris's manipulation of them in his works of the mid- to late-1960s is typical of what critic David Antin has described in other artists' works as simply a mannerist application of Modernist formulas. In retrospect, it is arguable that whatever may have seemed revolutionary in Minimal art was nothing more than the sensate delectation of the object in space—a temporal analogue to retinal art. See Morris's "Notes on Sculpture," part 1, *Artforum* 4 (February 1966): 42–44; part 2, *Artforum* 5 (October 1966): 20–23.

2. Robert Morris, *Robert Morris: Mirror Works 1961–78* (New York: Leo Castelli, Inc., 1979), n.p.

3. Robert Morris, "The Present Tense of Space," *Art in America* 66 (January/February 1978): 70.

4. Ibid., pp. 70–81.

5. Ibid., p. 80.

Dennis Oppenheim

Born in Mason City (now Electric City), Washington, September 6, 1938.
Lives in New York.

Education

B.F.A., California College of Arts and Crafts, Oakland, 1965.

M.A., Stanford University, Palo Alto, California, 1965.

Awards

Guggenheim Foundation Fellowship, 1971.

National Endowment for the Arts Artists Fellowship, 1974, 1981.

Selected Solo Exhibitions

John Gibson Gallery, New York, 1968–79.

Galerie Yvon Lambert, Paris, 1971, 1977.

Tate Gallery, London, 1972.

Sonnabend Gallery, New York 1972, 1973.

Museum of Conceptual Art, San Francisco, 1973.

Stedelijk Museum, Amsterdam, 1974.

Palais des Beaux-Arts, Brussels, 1975.

The Kitchen Center for Video, Music and Dance, New York, 1975, 1979.

M.L. D'Arc Gallery, New York, 1976, 1977.

Wright State University, Dayton, Ohio, 1977.

Musée d'Art Contemporain, Montreal, 1978, and tour, 1978–79.

Kunsthalle Basel, Switzerland, 1979.

Ace Gallery, Los Angeles, 1980.

Contemporary Arts Center, Cincinnati, 1980.

Portland (Oregon) Center for the Visual Arts, 1980.

Selected Group Exhibitions

Information, The Museum of Modern Art, New York, 1970.

Annual Exhibition, Whitney Museum of American Art, New York, 1970; *Biennial Exhibition,* 1977, 1981.

Words and Works, The Clocktower, Institute for Art and Urban Resources, New York, 1974.

Body Art, Museum of Contemporary Art, Chicago, 1975.

Venice Biennale, 1976, 1980.

Rooms, P.S.1, Institute for Art and Urban Resources, New York, 1976.

Time, Philadelphia College of Art, 1977.

Early Work by Five Contemporary Artists, The New Museum, New York, 1977.

Documents VI, Kassel, West Germany, 1977.

Narrative Art, Contemporary Arts Museum, Houston, 1978.

Concept, Narrative, Document, Museum of Contemporary Art, Chicago, 1979.

Image and Object in Contemporary Sculpture, The Detroit Institute of Arts, 1979.

Morris, Acconci, Oppenheim, Sonnabend Gallery, New York, 1980.

Architectural Sculpture, Los Angeles Institute of Contemporary Art, 1980.

Machineworks: Vito Acconci, Alice Aycock, Dennis Oppenheim, Institute for Contemporary Art, University of Pennsylvania, Philadelphia, 1981.

Mythos und Ritual in der Kunst der 70er Jahre, Kunsthaus Zürich, 1981.

Selected Bibliography

Alloway, Lawrence. *Topics in American Art Since 1945.* New York: W. W. Norton & Co., 1975.

Ashton, Dore. "Exercises in Anti-Style: Six Ways of Regarding Un, In, and Anti-Form." *Arts Magazine* 43 (April 1969): 45–47.

Baker, Kenneth. "Dennis Oppenheim: An Art with Nothing to Lose." *Arts Magazine* 49 (April 1975): 72–74.

Belloli, Jay. *Image and Object in Contemporary Sculpture,* exhibition catalog. Detroit: The Detroit Institute of Arts, 1979.

Braun, Emily. "Dennis Oppenheim: The Factories." *Arts Magazine* 55 (June 1981): 138–41.

Burnham, Jack. "The Artist as Shaman." *Arts Magazine* 47 (May–June 1973): 42–44.

———. "Real Time Systems." *Artforum* 8 (September 1969): 49–55.

Calas, Nicolas. "Madness in the Arena." *Artforum* 16 (September 1977): 51–53.

Celant, Germano. "Towards an Acritical Criticism." *Casabella* 33 (December 1969): 42–44.

Crary, Jonathan. "Dennis Oppenheim's Delirious Operations." *Artforum* 19 (November 1978): 36–40.

Dennis Oppenheim, exhibition catalog. Amsterdam: Stedelijk Museum, 1974.

Felshin, Nina. "Constructions II: Dennis Oppenheim." *Dialogue* 3 (March–April 1981): 19–21.

Fend, Peter. "New York, New York: Dennis Oppenheim." *Flash Art* 86–87 (January–February 1979): 42.

Frank, Peter. "The Arts in Fusion." *Dance Magazine* 48 (April 1974): 55–57.

Goldberg, Lenore. "Myth and Ritual: Lenore Goldberg Discusses the Work of Dennis Oppenheim." *Art and Artists* 8 (August 1973): 22–27.

———. "A Renewal of Possibilities." *Arts Magazine* 47 (March 1973): 33–37.

M. C. Akin

The Assembly Line. (With By-Products from a Mechanical Trance), 1980
Installation at The Portland Center for the Visual Arts, Portland, Oregon
High-powered blowers, vents, suspended tables, motorized metronome, fan supported by overhead boom, transparent air sacks on rotary rack, mobile shield with springs between plates, hatch openings into stage deck
22.9 × 4.3 × 10.1 (75 × 14 × 33)

Crystal Recorder. (Stroking the Throat of Tornado Diane). An Early Warning System, 1980
Installation at University of California, Irvine
One-third scale. Project designated for exterior location, United States.
Redwood, formica, glass, steel, cotton fabric, water, motorized pan, pulleys, rope, copper
4.9 × 3.6 × 2.4 (16 × 12 × 8)

Goldberg, RoseLee. *Performance: Live Art 1909 to the Present,* pp. 101–2. New York: Harry N. Abrams, 1979.

———. "Space as Praxis." *Studio International* 190 (September–October 1975): 130–35.

Goldin, Amy. "Sweet Mystery of Life." *Art News* 68 (May 1969): 46–51, 62.

Henri, Adrian. *Total Art: Environments, Happenings, and Performance.* New York: Praeger Publishers, 1977.

Herman, Jerry. "Arts Reviews: 3 Installations: Sonnabend." *Arts Magazine* 54 (June 1980): 33–34.

Hershman, Lynn. "Interview with Dennis Oppenheim." *Studio International* 186 (November 1973): 196–97.

Walter Drayer

Second Site for a Staircase, 1980
Installation at Musée d'Art et d'Histoire, Geneva
Canvas bellows on grinding wheels with carbon arc light mounted behind adjustable glass plates. Magnetic pendulum with six butane canisters, motorized rotating armature with fireworks (sparklers, rockets, and Roman candles), rotating central armature with fireworks and wax candles mounted between copper and galvanized cutting disks. Silvered reflector shields, suspended transparent drumskins mounted on mesh screens, copper launching stacks on casters with loading device supported by overhead boom.
15′ × 30′ × 60′

Hess, Thomas B. "Ceremonies of Measurements." *New York Magazine* 10 (March 21, 1977): 60–62.

Hickey, Dave. "Earthscapes, Landworks and Oz." *Art in America* 59 (September–October 1971): 40–49.

Jacobs, Jay. "The Iceman Cometh—Symptoms of the Seventies." *Art in America* 58 (January–February 1970): 62–67.

Johnson, Ellen H. *Modern Art and the Object: A Century of Changing Attitudes.* New York: Harper & Row Publishers, 1976.

Kaprow, Allan. "The Education of the Un-artist," part 1, *Art News* 69 (February 1971): 28–31, 66–68; part 2, *Art News* 71 (May 1972): 34–39, 62B–63.

Kardon, Janet. "Janet Kardon Interviews Some Modern Maze-Makers: Dennis Opienheim, September 1975." *Art International* 20 (April–May 1976): 66–67.

———. *Time,* exhibition catalog, p. 20. Philadelphia: Philadelphia College of Art, 1977.

Kozloff, Max. "Pygmalion Reversed." *Artforum* 14 (November 1975): 30–37.

Larson, Kay. "Metaphysical Attraction." *Village Voice,* March 17, 1980, p. 79.

Lippard, Lucy R. *Six Years: The Dematerialization of the Art Object from 1966 to 1972.* New York: Praeger Publishers, 1973.

Machineworks: Vito Acconci, Alice Aycock, Dennis Oppenheim, exhibition catalog. Philadelphia: Institute of Contemporary Art, University of Pennsylvania, 1981.

McShine, Kynaston L,, ed. *Information,* exhibition catalog, pp. 104–5. New York: The Museum of Modern Art, 1970.

Meyer, Ursula. *Conceptual Art,* pp. 196–99. New York: E. P. Dutton & Co., 1972.

Morgan, Stuart. "Reviews: Philadelphia: 'Machineworks, Institute of Contemporary Art.' " *Artforum* 19 (Summer 1981): 97–98.

Mythos und Ritual in der Kunst der 70er Jahre, exhibition catalog. Zurich: Kunsthaus Zürich, 1981.

Oppenheim, Dennis. "Catalyst 1967–1974." In *Individuals: Post-Movement Art in America,* edited by Alan Sondheim, pp. 246–66. New York: E. P. Dutton & Co., 1977.

———. "Interactions: Form-Energy-Subject." *Arts Magazine* 46 (March 1972): 36–39.

———. "Recurring Aspects in Sculpture." *Cover* 2 (January 1980): 36–39.

Parent, Alain. *Dennis Oppenheim, rétrospective de l'oeuvre 1967–1977; Retrospective—Works 1967–1977,* exhibition catalog. Montreal: Musée d'Art Contemporain, 1978.

Pincus-Witten, Robert. "Theatre of the Conceptual." *Artforum* 12 (October 1973): 40–46.

Schjeldahl, Peter. "Sculpture as Big as All Outdoors." *New York Times,* July 6, 1980, sec. 22, p. 10.

Schwartzman, Allan. "Dennis Oppenheim, an Interview by Allan Schwartzman." In *Early Work by Five Contemporary Artists: Ron Gorchov, Elizabeth Murray, Dennis Oppenheim, Dorothea Rockburne, Joel Shapiro,* exhibition catalog. New York: New Museum, 1977.

Sharp, Willoughby. "Dennis Oppenheim Interviewed by Willoughby Sharp." *Studio International* 182 (November 1971): 186–93.

———. "Dennis Oppenheim . . . Recall." *Avalanche Newspaper,* May–June 1974, pp. 14–15.

Situation Concepts, exhibition catalog. Innsbruck: Galerie im Taxispalais, 1971.

Spurlock, William, ed. *16 Projects/4 Artists: Laurie Anderson, Dennis Oppenheim, Michelle Stuart, William Wegman,* exhibition catalog. Dayton, Ohio: Wright State University, 1978.

Staniszewski, Mary Anne. "New York Reviews: Acconci, Morris, Oppenheim." *Art News* 79 (September 1980): 248–49.

Wood, Steve. "An Interview with Dennis Oppenheim." *Arts Magazine* 55 (June 1981): 133–37.

Wortz, Melinda. "University of California, Irvine." In *Architectural Sculpture: Projects,* exhibition catalog, pp. 38–44. Los Angeles: Los Angeles Institute of Contemporary Art, 1980.

Jim Rosenberger

Life-Support System for a Premature By-Product (From a Long Distance), 1981
Installation at Contemporary Arts Center, Cincinnati (two views)
Sonnabend Gallery, New York
Canvas bellows with glass keys mounted on steel ramp, pulley-operated vessel with steel masts operated under black enamel cymbals. Wooden launching ramps, motorized conveyor belt with steel-and-mesh cage supporting infrared butane heaters. Colored and transparent rubber hose, glass pipe and cylinders supported in steel grids and secured on mechanical jacks and sandblasted springs. Galvanized container with connecting pipes, induction fan with overhead rotating roller conveyor.
15′ × 40′ × 80′

The complex and fearsome constructions that Dennis Oppenheim has been creating since the late 1970s—aggressive transformers, powerplants, reactors, and conversion factories—seem caught in a state of perpetual agitation and restless energy. The energy that possesses his machines is the erratic and mysterious energy of artistic creation and of thought itself. Oppenheim sees this as an awesomely potent energy, capable of being transformed and transfused into many forms; the processes and by-products of its conversions are the subject of his art.

Oppenheim has theorized that "the energy which an artist puts into his work literally burns out as the object is made." He describes his recent projects as "in the service of dealing with art at its most potent moment—the moment of conception. I have attempted to reconstruct for myself," he continues, "the mental housing which represents the idea when it was strongest and most pure. The physical structures mirror the thought which produced them, allowing the exterior form to function at the same high energy plane as a thought traveling through the mind."[1] The "burn-out" of the artist's energy in the act of creation does not, as cited by Oppenheim, yield a quantum loss of energy in the world. Rather, the creative energy of the artist is converted into another mode, that of the constructed object. That the artist's vital energy and essence can be *converted,* and not just recorded or memorialized, into the art object; that the artist can somehow *become* his work, is a highly Romantic notion, and one amplified in Oppenheim's oeuvre through the insinuation of modern science which teaches that energy is convertible into matter and vice versa.

There can be no more appropriate form to represent this creative energy and its products than the morphology of the machine, itself a system or network of systems to harness energy and raw material for transformation into some other, synthetic, entity. "Machines," reflects Oppenheim, "are a rather perfect device to use as a metaphor for thinking. They have real-time as well as image and function parallels. Machines relate to our thought and biological processes. There are numerous inside/outside connections between the self and the morphology of machines and industrial systems that can be tapped as an art source."[2] Such "inside/outside connections" are a critical element for Oppenheim, because he sees his works not as stillborn, static, self-contained objects, but as active, dynamically functional enactments of the energy—the mental energy—that flows from the artist in the beginning to fuel them forever. In Oppenheim's work some mystical synapse between the idea and the object is perpetually bridged by what, according to the artist, is an *actual* transference of imaginative energy. Thus he can plausibly call his machines by such names as "hallucinations" and "solid forms of mechanical hysteria."[3]

Hallucination and mechanical hysteria are indeed fitting descriptions for *Launching Station # 1. An Armature for Projection.,* Oppenheim's project for the Hirshhorn Museum. In conversation he has repeatedly stressed the apparent danger of this physically massive and visually overwhelming "launching station," describing it variously as "willful," "unpredictable," and "on the threshold of going out of control."[4] Even at rest, this construction has the look of something unresponsive to human volition. In its fully activated state, the machine is in danger of literally going out of control: nearly a dozen motors are spinning (including a large central dynamo that whirls at terribly high speeds; an intense white light periodically erupts from a smoldering carbon arc lamp that ignites explosive powder dispersed from a vibrating metal plate; jets of flame erupt from trumpets and French horns and Roman candles shoot and ricochet about; fire and electricity are everywhere. In the Hirshhorn Museum installation the *Launching Station* is, for safety reasons, largely dormant or semi-operative, although the machine is in fact fully engineered to operate as described.)

The *Launching Station*—a fully mobile instrument, like the lunar landing module—is designed to be wheeled onto a frozen lake. Conceived as a combination sensing device/mining device/processing plant, the station has been designed to search out and extract some unspecified energy source deep under the ice. The most powerful and dominant of the three principal elements of the *Launching Station* is the "boring room," a large rotary device with a huge descending auger that drills through the comparatively frail ice. What the boring room dredges up it emits through a whirling set of glass tubes in a spew of white-hot sparks that are heated to super-temperatures by the intense flame erupting like a blowtorch jet from an ignition tower stationed nearby. Surrounding this circular boring apparatus is a round flat surface sloping into the center like a very broad funnel. Positioned on it radially at regular intervals is another bank of glass tubes, each of which has at its base a Roman candle poised for takeoff when contact is made with a series of igniting devices on the underside of the turning boring room. Encircling all of this is a cooling tank in the form of a water trough, equipped with two turning waterwheel-like affairs, one fitted with flares that burn under water and the other a rotating device with copper plates described by Oppenheim as a developing mechanism.

The boring room and its attendant fixtures, collectively the nexus of the launching station, are by far the most forbidding part of the construction. Oppenheim, for whom the structure retains as much mystery as it does for the viewer, describes the energy that radiates or is hurled from the boring device as so potent that "it must be observed through a screen and handled with tongs." There are no tongs, but this heart of the *Launching Station* is surrounded by a number of movable deflection screens (they resemble the long shields used by ancient Roman soldiers to march into battle) made of highly polished copper, each fitted with a single window made of cobalt-blue glass. These shields protect the viewer from the awesome potency of the creative energies dredged up from some unfathomable subconscious source; they also protect the viewer from the other operations conducted in and out of the boring area by the remaining major elements of the thought-conversion factory.

Servicing the boring operation is the second major component: a curved "projection ramp," fashioned

Launching Station #1. An Armature for Projection, 1981
Installation at Hirshhorn Museum and Sculpture Garden
Acetylene torch, aluminum, butane tanks, carbon arc lamp, copper, fans, fluorescent lights, galvanized sheet metal, gas burners, glass, luminous rocks, mirrors, motors, musical horns, pyrotechnical devices (firecrackers, flares, rockets, Roman candles), rubber, steel, water
Overall dimensions of site approx. 8.5 × 10.7 (28 × 35)

Entire structure is portable and mobile. The aerial projection is a hallucination emanating from the ground-based structure. It decodes the atomic structure of the launching apparatus itself and renders it visible in terms of thought transmission. The recording developing elements are active physical units in the work. In that way it is its own receiver.
—Dennis Oppenheim

from tubular metal elements, that rocks back and forth on a motorized scaffold. The ramp cradles an oblong, gemlike glass object that spits fire as it rolls along the length of the ramp, shuttling between the extended glass rods of the boring apparatus at one end and a fabrication zone at the other. The fabrication device, suspended from the ceiling above the far end of the ramp, consists of rotating steel discs which are cut by an acetylene torch into flat rings; as the rings are manufactured they become snared on the end of the rocking projection ramp. Flanking the ramp are two rocketry stations made of yet more curved-glass tubes; fitted in the base end of each tube is a Roman candle. As these fireworks are ignited by the pyrotechnical rolling glass container, they shoot through the curved glass tubes and are fired directly into the long surface of a rotating device suspended above the central ramp. The multifaceted surface of this component is clad with parabolic mirrors and copper plates which the artist describes as scanning and recording devices, as if they were photographic film. The rockets ricochet from these plates in many directions; some of them are deflected into the developing tank encircling the boring room, completing a kind of reflexive process, an

Launching Station #1

interplay between the operation of the boring room and that of an external, active stimulus.

The final major element of the station, described by Oppenheim as a wind machine, is a circular metal collar in which are implanted four very rapidly and very dangerously spinning fans. The device resembles a tambourine, except that it is probably lethal to the touch and is suspended from the ceiling and mounted over a spiral of copper tubing that looks like a tornado. The wind machine is connected to the boring center by a pair of perpendicular chutes. Above the chutes a vibrating metal plate showers luminous dust down to their tilted surfaces.

Detail of *Launching Station #1*

These are the major components of *Launching Station #1*. Together they delineate a complex matrix of symbiotic relationships, disjunctive activities, and accidental events. The station is an overwhelming barrage of visual metaphoric information, the assimilation and interpretation of which is made all the more difficult by the erratic and unpredictable manner in which the station—or its many parts—operates.

Precise explication of this wondrous mechanism is impossible; Oppenheim deliberately obscures, confuses, and confounds his concerns, replicating in his engines of thought the mystery and untamability of the creative process itself. Taken as a whole, this grand perceptual mechanism demonstrates the suprastructure of symbiotic and often random relationships that are creative thought; it is unnecessary to perceive in the anatomy of these machines an exact one-to-one relationship with some precise mental operation. The *Launching Station* is, after all, a "hallucination," "hysteria," expressed through the vocabulary of industrial apparatus.

As if to underscore this hallucinatory aspect, Oppenheim "indexes" his machine with an outsized kaleidoscope trained on it from a slightly removed observation point.[5] Inside the kaleidoscope are no bits of colored glass, but a mirror-and-lens construction through which the *Launching Station* is rendered as a dazzling, fractured image, an ambivalent visual evocation of either the spectacle of the machine at the full pitch of its creative urge, or the specter of the whole contraption

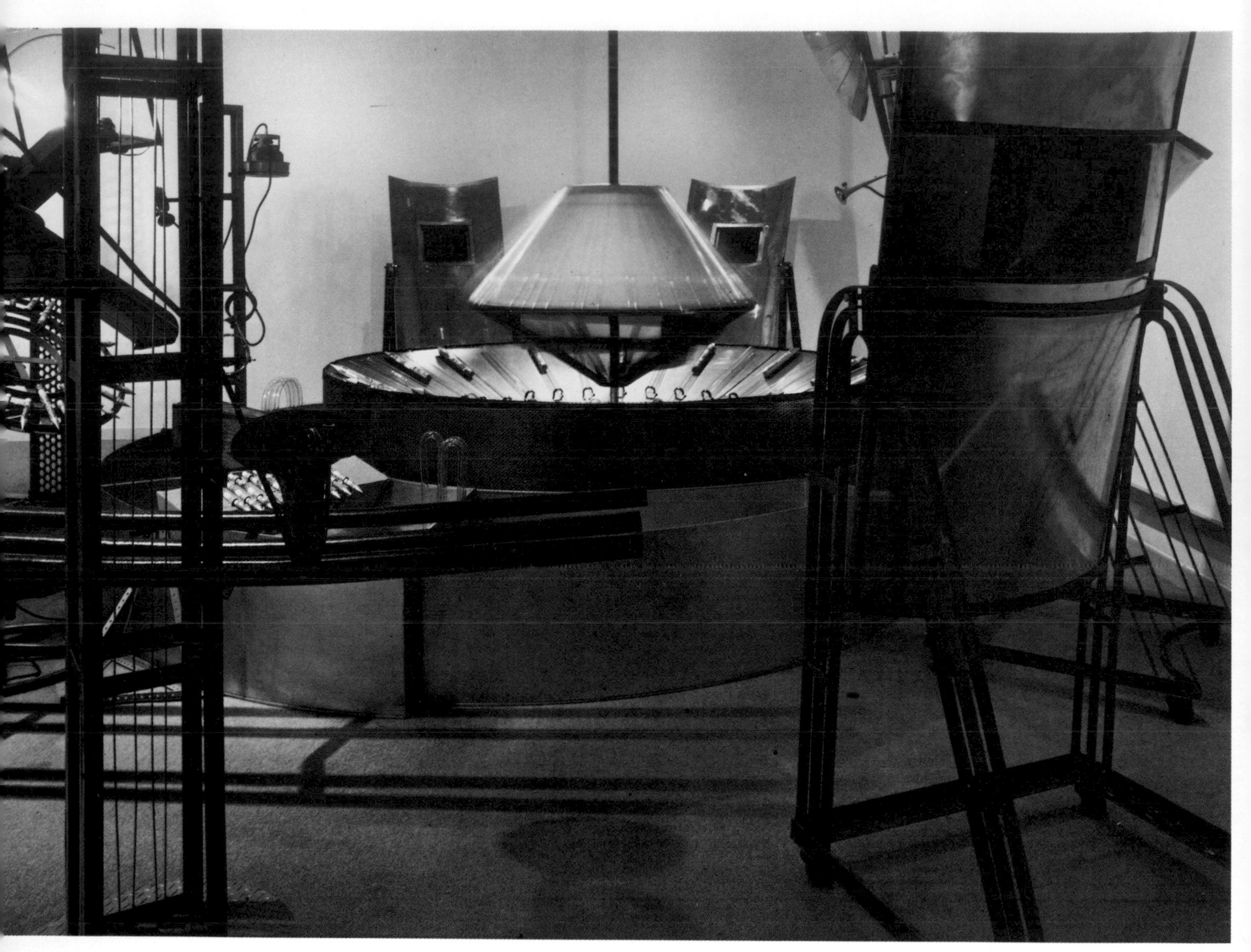

Detail of *Launching Station #1*

colliding, merging, and caving in on itself in a final, self-consuming meltdown.

In fact, Oppenheim has endowed his machine with what he explains as "both a 'hot' topology and a 'cold' one," meaning that the machine is sometimes dormant and sometimes highly active. The "down periods" suggest both the serenity of the mind at rest or the malfunctioning of the entire system—fallow periods, blocks, distractions, impasses, etc.[6] With the near-crazed *Launching Station* everywhere triggered for action—its rotors spinning, its many missiles poised for firing, its conveyor belt and wind machine churning—this apparatus chronically poses the risk of catastrophe. It is certainly possible that the machine might self-destruct in an out-of-control frenzy. In such an event, it would not become less of a metaphor but only a somewhat altered one, connoting a different psychic (or mortal) condition. But Oppenheim's metaphor is one of conductivity in the active, creative mind. In his vision it is essential that the *capacity* of the machine for violent self-destruction or exhaustion be understood, that its susceptibility and vulnerability to burnout be known, but not that it be played out as an actual scenario. For these machines to burn out would short-circuit that very imaginative process which they are deployed to catalyze. Oppenheim simply refuses to make it that easy for his machines; the advent of such an ignominious destiny is far too nihilistic for an artistry founded on the very notion of a creative energy. Oppenheim's machines stand as a testament to the indomitability of the creative spirit. It is the uneasy fate of these machines, like that of the human imagination which they both galvanize and represent, to be caught eternally between their laborious travail and the consummation of their desire.

Notes

1. Dennis Oppenheim, "Dennis Oppenheim: Recurring Aspects in Sculpture," *Cover* 2 (January 1980): 36.
2. Steve Wood, "An Interview with Dennis Oppenheim," *Arts Magazine* 55 (June 1981): 133.
3. Ibid., pp. 135, 136.
4. These and subsequent uncited statements by Oppenheim are from conversations with the author in February, September, and November, 1981.
5. Because of space limitations, the kaleidoscope is not used in the Hirshhorn installation.
6. Within Oppenheim's oeuvre, such malfunctions of the creative process have deen a recurrent theme, in works such as *An Attempt to Raise Hell* (1974), *Early Morning Blues* (1976–77), *Ghost Town* (1979), and others.

Detail of *Launching Station #1*

EXIT

This catalog was designed by Carol Hare,
typeset by Carver Photocomposition, Inc.,
and printed by Wolk Press, Inc.
It was produced by the Smithsonian Institution Press,
Washington, D.C.,
for the Hirshhorn Museum and Sculpture Garden,
to accompany the exhibition
Metaphor: New Works by Contemporary Sculptors.